D0249667

A committed Christian, Nick is passionate about explaining complex topics in a simple way, yet without dumbing down. Nick has three Masters degrees and is currently reading for a doctorate in Islamic Studies at the University of Oxford. He has a business background, including at McKinsey. This is his first book. For more information see www.onestopguide.org.

REACHING MUSLIMS

A One-Stop Guide for Christians

Nick Chatrath

MONARCH
BOOKS

Oxford, UK & Grand Rapids, Michigan, USA

Copyright © 2011 by Nick Chatrath.

The right of Nick Chatrath to be identified as author of this work has been asserted by him in accordance with the Copyright, Designs and Patents Act 1988.

First published in the UK in 2011 by Monarch Books
(a publishing imprint of Lion Hudson plc)
Wilkinson House, Jordan Hill Road, Oxford OX2 8DR, England
Tel: +44 (0)1865 302750 Fax: +44 (0)1865 302757
Email: monarch@lionhudson.com
www.lionhudson.com

ISBN 978 0 85721 014 2

Distributed by:
UK: Marston Book Services, PO Box 269, Abingdon, Oxon, OX14 4YN
USA: Kregel Publications, PO Box 2607, Grand Rapids, Michigan 49501

The text paper used in this book has been made from wood independently certified as having come from sustainable forests.

British Library Cataloguing Data
A catalogue record for this book is available from the British Library.

Printed and bound in the UK by CPI Cox & Wyman, Reading.

The journey of this book

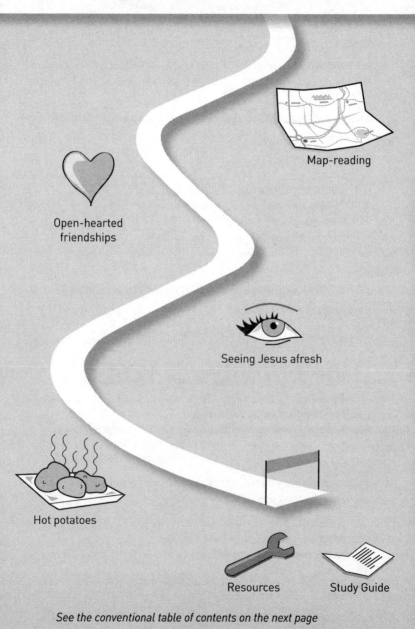

Map-reading

Open-hearted
friendships

Seeing Jesus afresh

Hot potatoes

Resources

Study Guide

See the conventional table of contents on the next page

Contents

Part 4 Hot potatoes: Some questions arising for Christians on aspects of Islam

Foreword

It is a privilege and a pleasure to commend Nick Chatrath's book. I was not prepared for how much I would enjoy it, not to mention how much information and wisdom it contains. I know of no book like this. It is long overdue. It is a handbook for Christians who need direction on how to approach Muslims. Nick's book will help you grasp the essentials of Islam and the intricacies of the Muslim mind and will show you how to converse with people like this in a very short period of time.

My own interest in this subject was whetted by my surprising relationship with the late President Yasser Arafat. I began praying daily for him in 1982, never expecting to meet him, but in 2002 Canon Andrew White took me into Ramallah when Arafat was very discouraged after the Israelis had bulldozed his compound. What might have been a fifteen-minute perfunctory visit lasted one hour and forty-five minutes. To say we "bonded" would be an overstatement, but something did happen between us that persevered through five extraordinary visits right up to his death.

Our conversations were almost entirely theological. I stressed one thing: that Jesus *died on the cross for our sins*. He said to me, "We believe that Jesus ascended into heaven." I replied: "But he died first, Rais, was raised from the dead and *then* ascended into heaven." He reached for his Quran, showing me (as if I could read Arabic) where the only woman mentioned in it was the Virgin Mary. I said, "So the Quran says Jesus was the Son of God – since he had no earthly father!" Dr Saeb Erekat, the chief negotiator for the Palestinians, was present and stressed that Jesus was a "prophet". I replied: "That's not good enough: he was the Son of God."

Had not Arafat been holed up in Ramallah – and feeling very low – it is unlikely I would have had so much time with him or that I would have got away with such candid discussions. I only know that I loved him – he felt it – and I did my best to present the gospel to him. It also sparked a deep interest in me to reach Muslims.

This is why I was so thrilled with Nick Chatrath's book. If only I had had the knowledge it provides when I visited Arafat. But we can all have it now, and I guarantee that you too will thank God for this book. It is absolutely brilliant. If your desire is to reach a Muslim for Jesus Christ, this is your book. I cannot imagine a better book on this subject: utterly compelling, it is as good as it gets. It shows essential knowledge for a Christian that they understand Islam. Yet it is written with moving compassion for Muslims. Churches should use this book to teach Christians about Islam and how to reach a Muslim. I pray for its wide distribution.

Dr R. T. Kendall

Senior Minister of Westminster Chapel, London, 1977–2002

Introduction

Tens of millions of Muslims live in the West. As a group they are ethnically diverse, culturally rich, and often wonderfully passionate about life and faith.

The problem is that as Christians we often segregate our lives from them. Many fear getting to know Muslims or – worse – are inherently suspicious. What a shame, since we live in a day of unprecedented opportunities to interact with Muslims from around the world!

This book will help you bridge the divide. If you are a Christian, what you have to share with Muslims is magnificent and potentially life-changing – Jesus really is great news for everyone! If you have zero knowledge about Islam and zero relationships with Muslims, don't worry: this book is for you. Think of it as a one-stop-shop introductory guide that will help you get to grips with the basics quickly. I am convinced that reaching Muslims is something we can all do, because fundamentally it involves friendship.

Various excellent books have been written in recent years about Islam and Muslims, including some from non-Muslim perspectives. Some of these books are also short. For example, Patrick Sookhdeo's brilliant *A Christian's Pocket Guide to Islam* focuses on beliefs and practices. And *Islam* and *Islamic History* (in the Oxford University Press *Very Short Introductions* series) deal in depth with historical and political issues. So why another book? I feel something else is needed that, as well as being concise, covers a broad range of aspects of Islam clearly and in a practical way. Islam is much more than just one thing, whether that thing is beliefs, practices, history, or politics. It is all these things, but Islam is also a story, an identity, a faith, a culture, and a social and demographic phenomenon. (In fact, it is a set of stories, a set of identities, and so on.) This book will try to reflect something of the diversity that exists among Muslims in all these dimensions.

I write as a Christian and primarily address Christians in English-speaking and/or Western countries, especially the UK, the USA, Canada, Europe, South Africa, Australia, and New Zealand. Others (including Muslims) are welcome to listen in, and will, I think, find Parts 1, 3, and 4 particularly interesting. But why is an introduction to Islam, specifically aimed at Christians, needed at all? In addition to the above, followers of Jesus will be interested in knowing how to communicate their faith to Muslims around them and how to relate with Muslims in ways that authentically follow Jesus' example.

As the "Picture of contents" page indicates, the four parts of this book deal with maps, hearts, eyes, and hot potatoes! Part 1 provides several maps of Islam – a crash course, if you like, in understanding the rich diversity of Islam and Muslims. The maps are: Stories and histories; Identity; Beliefs; Culture and practices; Politics and justice; and Demographics. You might like to think of Islam as the stage in a theatre. Each chapter in Part 1 is like a different stage light, with each shedding light at a particular angle onto the stage. Part 2 is focused on helping you to connect with Muslims. Here, I am eager to inspire you to develop open-hearted friendships with Muslims. After addressing at the most important obstacle for many – fear – there are chapters in Part 2 that will help you develop trust with Muslims you meet. Muslims love Jesus, and their view of him is different from that of Christians. So Part 3 considers various ways for Christians to communicate why Jesus is good news for them. Part 4 deals with three hot-potato issues that often arise in Christian discussions about reaching out to Muslims: the use of the word "Allah", when and whether one should baptize Christian believers from Muslim backgrounds, and whether Christians should eat halal meat. The study guides are there to help you apply this book in a group setting. The "Useful resources" section at the back is themed by topic so that you can easily find a book or website relevant to your area of interest. This book contains lots of notes, which mainly help track down further references. However, the book makes sense as a unit without the notes, so feel free to ignore them.

Because of the advice and correction of friends, this book is ten times better than it would have been. The idea for this book arose after I was asked by David Stroud and Mick Taylor to write a theological paper on Islam for their theological forum. I am grateful to Mick and David for the idea and for your encouragement in respect to this project. A particular thank you to Nicole Ashton for helping with study guides and workflow. In addition to those cited in the text, thank you to other members of the theology forum and to Kez Brennan, David Devenish, Harry Munt, Matt Partridge and Toby Skipper for reading (parts of) earlier versions of the text. Any remaining flaws and errors in this book are my own. Finally, thank you Tanja for listening to me ramble on endlessly about this book, and for helping me keep it vivid and to the point.

Part 1

Map-reading: What is Islam, and who are Muslims?

I moved house in 2005 to Oxford in the UK. I hardly knew the city, so when I received the keys to the house one of the first things I did was get a map. But what kind? A road map would have helped me find my way around. A tourist map would have pointed me to the colleges and museums. A map of bus or cycle routes would also have given me important information. Although the various maps have things in common, they are also quite different. And although each kind of map is accurate in its own way, none of them will tell you everything. (I ended up buying a road map, by the way.)

Similarly, although Muslims have much in common, the differences are also huge. Part 1 contains six maps, each of which introduces an aspect of Islam or Muslims. Taken together, the maps illustrate the extreme diversity to be found among Muslims. The maps are not exhaustive and their scopes overlap, in the same way that, for example, a street map may contain some, but not all, points of historical interest also contained in a tourist map.

Or to change the analogy, think about a precious jewel with many facets. Every Muslim is multifaceted, and this section will help you avoid reducing Islam or Muslims to any one of those facets, such as beliefs or practices.

I cannot underline enough the importance of getting to grips with maps like those in this section of the book. The value of what you will learn is not just in information gathering. These maps will help you ask good questions of Muslims, which will help you connect with them much more effectively. If we are excited about who Jesus is and what he has revealed (and as Christians we should be), surely the value of such connection is massive!

Before we proceed with these maps, two introductory points. First, a warning about generalizations. Many of us get most of our information about Islam from the media. But how accurate is what the media says about Christianity? None of us likes to be pigeon-holed. For example, in recent years the media has widely reported stories of child abuse associated with some members of the Roman Catholic Church, especially in the USA and Europe. Do Roman Catholic Christians, let alone other Christians, want to be tarred with this brush, as if all Christians acted like this and approved of it? Is this really representative of the behaviour of Catholics generally? Of course not. Similarly, we must resist most generalizations (good and bad) about Muslims, including cases where some hold views and have done things of which we would not approve. For this reason, each map that follows illustrates some things that are common among Muslims and some things that differ.

Second, the maps that follow describe aspects of Muslim worldviews. The Oxford English Dictionary defines "worldview" as a particular philosophy or view of life. Another way of thinking of a worldview is that it is a pair of glasses through which we view the world. Those glasses may include cultural, doctrinal, social, and other rules, but – and here's the key – everyone has a worldview, and it affects how we behave. As we consider what the various maps tell us about Islam and Muslims, remember that a Muslim's worldview will affect his or her behaviour. To put it another way, every one of the maps that follow affects what Muslims do.

Chapter 1

Stories and histories

What stories do Muslims tell? This chapter addresses two main kinds of story: ones about the past and, first, ones about the present. Here is a sample of stories that Muslims tell others and each other today:[1]

- My family's struggle. "You can't imagine the war zones we fled from and the financial difficulties we have faced. It hasn't been easy to make our way in life, or to be a Muslim, in such a non-Muslim society, especially one which is suspicious of us. The most important thing is to provide for our children and grandchildren, to give them a chance in life."

- Family is everything. "Although we live across three apartments, all my extended family is close by – grandfather, grandmother, three uncles, two aunts, husband, four children, and one daughter-in-law. I have a lot of love in my life.Amid the turmoil of our nation and world, family is the stable centre of our lives."[2]

- My parents just don't get it. This is a common story among teenagers and those in their twenties. It can work in two very different ways. "Islam is too serious; I just want to have some fun." Or, "My parents aren't morally observant; I'm returning to a pure, proper form of Islam." This last quote will come across as counter-intuitive to those who view teens and twenties as lazy, unfocused and apathetic. But a considerable number of young Muslims are fervent about their faith. For example, the influence of extremist student Islamic reform movements in some universities is very strong. A clear, purposeful call to teenagers to be serious about Islamic observance can seem inspiring to them, especially when presented in combination with the next two stories.

- Victim. "9/11 has really put pressure on us, not because we're Pakistani, but as Muslims. Government's always questioning everything we do these days: what goes on in mosques, in homes, in schools – everywhere. It's like, as Muslims, we're Public Enemy Number One. It gets to you. It's bound to get to you. You try to shrug it off, but it keeps coming back at you, keeps getting worse."[3] In many cases the stories of Islam are against "the West" or "Western oppressors". For many Muslims Western equals Christian. I have heard the language of victimhood (and expression of related feelings) from educated and less educated Muslims alike. Whether this is a real discrimination is not the point. When felt, the sense of being a victim is powerful. Add to this media reporting about Islamophobia and minority identity, and you have fuel on the fire of a sense of separateness. When beginning to get to know Muslims, remember that if you are a Westerner you may be in goodwill overdraft before you begin.

- Social glue. "I volunteer my time to Muslim Global Relief, get health advice from the Muslim Health Network, and make charitable donations to the Babylon Academy so that others can learn Arabic. My children go to Muslim schools along with many others on my street, and my son has a prayer timetable on his iPhone. Last month, shortly after my youngest was born, we conducted the shaving of the head ceremony, followed by having an animal sacrificed and distributed among friends, family, and the poor. Every now and then, I join my Muslim brothers to eat together in the community hall next to the mosque, especially in the evenings during Ramadan. Two of the most important meals we share together as a community are Eid al-Fitr and Eid al-Adha."[4]

- Islam as power against evil. "The evil eye in my taxi keeps me safe. By placing a plaque with words from the Quran above the door of my house, I ensure my family is protected against demons." For some Muslims, Islam functions as a more or less well defined protection mechanism.

- What a glorious past we have. "Stories of the Prophet Muhammad give me inspiration and guidance and give our community a sense of identity. The expansion of the Islamic empire in the decades following Muhammad's death shows the power of Islam. The rich civilizations Muslims produced are proof of Islam's greatness, which laid the foundations for the best of Western civilization today. Even amid the dark challenges of history such as the Crusades and the Mongol conquests, Muslims could not be kept down. We survived, flourished, and rose to positions of influence once more."

- Power and confidence. "We are rich and have returned to the pure roots of our faith. The West is decadent, sexually promiscuous, and morally corrupt. Islam has always been strong enough to expand. We are here to stay, growing in numbers and influence."

- I am part of a global community of believers. "I have a common bond with my Muslim brothers and sisters. When they were attacked in Bosnia, Sudan, Iraq, and Afghanistan, I felt their pain and suffering." Muslims are generally very aware of stories relating to fellow Muslims in other parts of the world. The strength of solidarity between Western Muslims and non-Western ones can often surprise non-Muslims, and the *umma* (the Islamic term for the global community of believers) is a key part of the reason for that solidarity.

Some of these stories are whispered quietly. Others are shouted for all to hear. Whatever the volume, the impact of such stories is deafening. One of the delightful things about stories is that you can't neatly put them in a box.[5] Whether in closed communities or out in the open in the public sphere, narrative has a way of shaping and influencing us extremely strongly, often in ways we cannot predict.

In order to understand your Muslim neighbour, college friend, or work colleague well, ask about the stories that have shaped and currently shape his or her life. Don't be afraid of doing this. We all have stories to tell. Say things like, "Tell me about your children," or, "What do you think about how Muslims are perceived?" Muslims will not bite your head off. They are friendly, generous, hospitable, hurting, wonderful people – in short, in many ways just like you and me.

Many of the above stories are related to the stories of early Islam. (You might call this "histories of Islam".) Although Islam is very varied, most versions of it flow from common roots relating to the Quran, Muhammad, and early Muslims.[6] The stories of Muhammad and the early Muslims (see boxes) are extremely important to most Muslims.

Muhammad

The early life of Muhammad, born in Mecca (in what is now Saudi Arabia) in roughly AD 570, gave little clue to the impact he would have as founder of the Muslim faith. To the north, the competing Byzantine and Sasanian empires were slowly disintegrating. In his early twenties, Muhammad married the wealthy widow Khadija. When meditating at Mount Hira (this was not uncommon locally), Muhammad was said to have been summoned to his calling as a prophet by the Angel Gabriel. In the next twelve years (610–622), Muhammad was in Mecca, where, apart from among his family and close friends, there was little positive response to his preaching. Next, Muhammad moved to Medina (also in what is now Saudi Arabia), where he became a figure of significant influence in Arabia and where more people pledged allegiance to Muhammed and what he stood for, including some who came from Mecca. Muhammad lived in Medina until his death in 632.

Early Muslims

Muhammad's death left his followers divided as to how succession should work and who should succeed him as leader of the early Muslim community. It is not inconceivable that the old Arabian tribes could have returned to their previous practices and governance structures rather than continue to demonstrate real allegiance to the emerging Muslim community. As it turned out, successive leaders called "caliphs" (the Arabic means "successors") took charge.

The first four caliphs were known as "rightly guided": they were Abu Bakr (ruled 632-634), Umar (634-644), Uthman (644-656) and Ali (656-661). Their reigns were all filled with turmoil (especially over the subject of the succession) and sowed seeds of conflict that have affected Islamic societies ever since. For example, Umar's forces conquered Jerusalem in 638. This event was preceded by bloodshed, with monasteries and villages destroyed.[7] By 661 the Muslim community had expanded to include much of North Africa, the Middle East, the Caucasus and most of Anatolia (present-day Turkey).

As well as asking your Muslim friends about their current life story, ask them about their understanding of the stories of early Islam. Maybe they will surprise you and talk about a story completely different to any that are mentioned above.

Everyone is multifaceted. Stories that Muslims tell are just one feature of who they are.

To end this chapter, the box below is for the more technically minded and highlights some of the historical difficulty we have in knowing about the early decades of Islam.

ADVANCED

A HISTORICAL PINCH OF SALT

What we know about Islam in its early decades (i.e. the mid-600s AD) is a subject of dispute. For example, Western scholars have in the past debated the early dating of the Quran, whether Islam really started in Arabia, and even the existence of Muhammad. Part of the problem is that there are very few materials dating from this period external to Muslim sources that back up much of the narrative traditionally accepted by Muslims. Key Muslim sources such as the major hadith collections (which contain reports of what Muhammad is said to have spoken and done) were put together more than 200 years after the death of Muhammad.

We can be fairly certain of a historical core that probably did happen, for example that Muhammad lived in Mecca, then went to Medina and somehow won back the support of the Meccans. Traditional Muslim accounts of the origins of Islam include many more specifics, some including degrees of detail such as Muhammad's recommendation that the right shoe be put on first. Those scholars using the best techniques of historical analysis generally accept that there was a period of development during which Islam came to take on the forms which are recognizable today. Nevertheless, traditional Muslim accounts are widely held in the Muslim community, and it is important to understand and appreciate them for what they are.

Chapter 2

Identity

How do you think most of your friends would answer the question, "Who are you?"? In response to the question asking them their religion in the 2001 UK census, 72 per cent of people put "Christian". In 2008, the American Religious Identification Survey found that the comparable figure for the USA was 76 per cent.[8] However, how many of the 72 per cent (or 76 per cent) would answer, "I am a Christian" if you asked them, "Who are you?"? The average Joe or Jane Bloggs in the West is more likely to self-identify as Welsh, Texan or an eco-warrior than to connect their identity in an unprompted way with their stated religion. For many in the West, our identity relates more strongly to things like our job, the city we come from or our political views.

The situation is very different for most Muslims. Ask a Muslim, "Who are you?" and it would not be surprising to get the answer, "I am a Muslim." In one sense this is natural, since in many Muslim nations identity cards include a field recording what religion you belong to. Also, because many Muslims in the West see themselves as living as a minority in a "Christian country", they may be more likely to use the term "Muslim" to describe their identity. In my experience, even nominal Muslims are likely to attach great importance to being known as a Muslim.[9]

For most Muslims, the fact that they are Muslims is at the heart of who they see themselves to be.

In constructing a map of Muslim identity, then, we must recognize that the point in the above paragraph is held in common among most Muslims. But now consider the differences. For those with a radical, extremist interpretation of the Quran ("the fundamentalists"), one's identity as a Muslim is much more important than any claims of ethnicity, political view, and social standing. At the other end of the spectrum are Muslims like Tariq Ramadan. In a talk on identity in 2007, he said, "I am a Muslim, I am Swiss, I am European, I am an academic."[10] We might call this a "very West-friendly" approach. This is a multidimensional view of identity consistent with Tariq Ramadan's desire to reform Islam. Between these two approaches are "mainstream Muslims" who, while not actively seeking reformation of the practice of Islam (be it fundamentalist or liberal reformation), see their identity as Muslims of a particular ethnic and cultural background (for example, Pakistani Muslims who left Pakistan after the Partition of India in 1947). For some Iranian and Arab Muslims, national and linguistic differences are important markers of deeper cultural and historical divides. For other Muslims such differences, far from being a problem, are to be celebrated.

Understanding various Muslim views on identity is important because it helps us understand the different kinds of questions they are asking. For example, fundamentalists may ask first, "What can we do to bring about the immediate imposition of *shari'a* law where we live?" Those taking a "very West-friendly" approach are more likely to ask, "How can we become better American, Dutch, or British Muslims?", or "How can our society become more tolerant?" Mainstream Muslims might start by asking, "Where can I find a good Muslim school for my children?" and "Why does the West hate Muslims?" – and many more questions besides. The points of contact with each kind of Muslim will vary.

So when you meet Muslims for the first time, ask them about their family background. If they or their family recently moved to the West, ask them about their views on living in this country. As you do this, know that although religious identity is important for most Muslims, the answers you get to these questions will probably vary greatly from Muslim to Muslim.

Everyone is multifaceted. How Muslims view their identities is just one aspect of who they are.

Chapter 3

Beliefs

Trying to summarize Muslim beliefs in a few pages is a daunting task. Even more so when I am trying to illustrate both commonalities and differences among Muslims. Inevitably, I have had to be selective. Readers who want to know more should consult the thematically categorized resources list in Appendix 2.

For the vast, vast majority of Muslims, anyone not holding to the beliefs outlined in the next two boxes is not a Muslim.[11]

What Muslims believe[12]

Muslims believe in one God (Allah), his complete authority over human destiny, life after death, and a day of judgment. Allah is merciful, but Muslims have no assurance of receiving his mercy on the day of judgment. They believe in a chain of prophets starting with Adam and including Jesus. They also believe that God's final message to humankind was revealed to the Prophet Muhammad through Gabriel in Arabic and recorded word for word in the Quran. The five pillars (see below) are key beliefs and practices that, according to Muslim belief, Muslims must uphold.

The five pillars of Islam

The creed (*Shahada*): "There is no God but God [Allah], and Muhammad is his messenger." It is the sincere recitation of this creed, in the presence of a witness, that makes one a Muslim.

Fasting (*Sawm*): With some exceptions (e.g. pregnant women), Muslims should not eat, drink, smoke, or have sex during daylight hours in the month of Ramadan.

Giving to the poor (*Zakat*): Muslims are expected to give 2.5 per cent of their income.

Prayer (*Salat*): There are five sets of Arabic prayers per day that are required, and more that are optional. Muslims pray in the direction of Mecca.

Pilgrimage to Mecca (*Hajj*): All Muslims who are physically able and who have the money to do so are expected to go on pilgrimage to Mecca at least once during their lifetime. Muslims consider that giving money to help other Muslims go on pilgrimage gains them (the giver) merit with God.

Another point of widespread agreement among Muslims is that beliefs matter for life. Who I bank with, when I pray, what I eat, where I send my daughter to school, how I punish a thief: all this and more is governed by stipulations of Islamic tradition and law, even if different Muslims interpret the various stipulations differently.

There are many important sources of beliefs for Muslims, the best known and most revered of which is the Quran (see box).

The Quran

The Quran is a book in Arabic containing 114 sections (each section is called a *sura*), arranged in approximately descending order of length. The Quran is approximately the same length as the New Testament in the Bible. Each *sura* has a name – the first four translate as "The Opening", "The Cow", "The House of Imran", and "Women". A *sura* is made up of verses – a verse is known as an *aya*. The Quran includes stories, excerpts from stories, poetry, and doctrinal instruction, among other genres.

Traditional Islamic teaching holds that over a period of about twenty-three years (between approximately AD 610 and 632), the angel Gabriel revealed successive portions of the Quran to Muhammad. Most scholars believe that the version of the Quran we have today is that put together by Uthman later in the seventh century. Muslims believe that God revealed the Quran by dictation with 100 per cent accuracy via Gabriel to Muhammad.[13]

Muslims differ about various aspects of the Quran, including how and when it was put together, the status of verses alleged to be in previous versions but then omitted later, how it should be pronounced, and how to relate seemingly contradictory verses to each other. Some of these differences came to be reflected in different "schools of law", the main Sunni ones being known as Hanafi, Maliki, Shafi'i, and Hanbali.[14]

Some Muslims disagree about almost every other belief. Beliefs about Christianity illustrate this. For example, almost all Muslims give a high place to Jesus, believing him to have been a prophet born of a virgin. The Quran names him as (among other things) "Messiah". But whereas most Muslims do not believe Jesus was crucified at the cross, the Ahmadiyyas believe that he was, but then revived and went to live in India.[15]

Some Muslim and Christian beliefs compared

Points of agreement between Muslims and Christians:
- Belief in one God and in the existence of angels and the devil.
- Acceptance of the books of Moses, the Psalms, and the Gospels as the Word of God (although Muslims generally think the version Christians now have has been corrupted).
- Belief that prophets are inspired by God and give messages from God.
- Belief in the day of resurrection and judgment and the existence of heaven and hell.
- The importance of fasting, helping the poor and community.

Points of disagreement between Muslims and Christians:
- Muslims believe that Jesus was a prophet of God. Christians believe that Jesus was a prophet of God and also "God who became man", the one who died on the cross to reconcile people with God.
- Muslims believe that entry to paradise (heaven) is mainly by virtue of one's good actions outweighing one's bad actions. Christians believe that salvation (which includes entry to heaven) is a gift received by faith in Jesus Christ – a gift made possible by Jesus' actions, with our changed actions as evidence of having received this gift.
- Muslims believe that God is one and not three. Christians believe that God is three in one.
- Christians believe that God dwells with his people. Muslims do not believe this.

Here are some examples of Islamic beliefs on which Muslims differ:
- Shi'i Muslims hold that members of Muhammad's family and his descendants (variously defined, depending on what kind of Shi'i you are) are the rightful spiritual and political rulers of

Islam, starting with Ali, Muhammad's cousin and son-in-law. By contrast, Sunni Muslims consider Ali to have been the fourth leader of the Muslim community after Muhammad.[16]

- Sufi Muslims advocate using tombs of saints as places of worship and approve of dancing and getting into states of ecstasy in a worship context, whereas Wahhabi Muslims denounce all this as heretical.[17] It is possible to be both Sufi and Sunni or both Sufi and Shi'i.

- Some Muslims hold a mixture of animist and Islamic beliefs. These Muslims are sometimes known as folk Muslims, although they would rarely use that term themselves. Examples of typical folk Muslim practices are using Quranic verses as charms and hanging the evil eye to ward off danger. Such practices often exert a very powerful hold over the Muslims who do them. In many cases, the belief in the strength of charms is not so much intellectual as rooted in binding habits that have become part of life. Many other Muslims denounce such practices.

- Muslims generally agree that it is good to follow the examples of Muhammad and his first companions. Not following such examples is counted as *bid'a* (innovation), but Muslims differ on what specific views and practices should be counted as *bid'a* today. This is illustrated in the discussion among Muslims about whether it was right to put a bounty on the head of British-Indian writer Salman Rushdie.[18]

- Views on violence vary widely among Muslims. Some love and seek peace, believing it to be central to their faith. Others resist condemning violence such as that perpetrated on 9/11 or 7/7, or even go so far as to glorify such violence (see box below). Many surveys have been done on the levels of support for extremism among Muslims, not all with consistent results, so it is difficult to draw definitive conclusions. For example, among American Muslims who think of themselves as Muslims first, only 28 per cent believe that groups of Arabs carried out the 9/11 attacks.

However, among American Muslims who think of themselves as Americans first, the figure rises to 61 per cent.[19] In the UK, another survey showed that half of British Muslims aged 18–24 believe America and Israel were responsible for 9/11.[20]

Differing Muslim reactions to 9/11

"The people at this conference look at September 11 like a battle, as a great achievement by the mujahideen [fighters] against the evil superpower." (Meeting of Muslim Clerics, Finsbury Park, 11 September 2002)[21]

"British Muslims, along with everyone else, are watching events in America with shock and horror. Whoever is responsible for these dreadful, wanton attacks, we condemn them utterly." (The Muslim Council of Britain, press release 11 September 2001)[22]

Beware a little knowledge. You might assume that no Muslim values a close relationship with God but then meet a postmodern or Sufi Muslim who values exactly that. Keep in mind that there are probably as many different approaches to Islam as there are Muslims. Also, steer well clear of simplistic statements such as "Islam is wrong". That statement misses the point, because there are so many different and conflicting aspects to Islamic belief. Worse, any Muslim who hears this might think, "But I give to the poor and am hospitable. That is what Islam means to me. Clearly this individual thinks that giving to the poor is wrong."

Given the divergence in views among Muslims today, one might be forgiven for asking: are there several Islams today, even hundreds or millions of different Islams? Almost all Muslims will tell you "No", and we should accept this at face value – it is not the role of non-Muslims to define Islam for Muslims. What you should and must do, if you are to find out about Muslim beliefs, is ask for yourself.

As you get to know Muslims, remember that there are some beliefs you will agree on and some things you will disagree on. But do not be afraid of asking your Muslim friends what they believe, why they believe it, and how they square that with other Muslim beliefs. In my experience, they are happy to respond.

Everyone is multifaceted. What Muslims believe is just one facet of who they are.

Chapter 4
Cultures and practices

"In a December 2005 Gallup poll of American households, when Americans were asked what they most admire about Muslim societies, the answer 'nothing' was the most frequent response. The second most frequent response? 'I don't know.' Combined, these two responses represented the majority (57%) of Americans surveyed."[23]

I am unsure whether I am more shocked or disgusted when I read the above quotation. There is much to admire in Muslim societies. Not that Muslim societies are perfect, but there are things to applaud. Such societies are often characterized by hospitality and an emphasis on family and community. Historically, Muslim civilizations have made some advances in areas such as architecture, maths, astronomy, art, and calligraphy. It is vital to realize that there are positive aspects of Muslim culture and practice.

In this vast area[24] Muslims hold much in common. The practice of prayer is one example. Muslims will often refer to "doing prayers", rather than "saying prayers". Prayer is generally composed of a number of cycles that involve moving into different positions, for example prostration.

The box below illustrates the close relationships between Islamic prayer practices and Islamic beliefs about prayer. In other words, this map and the preceding one are closely related.

Other practices may more accurately be called habits or norms and are held in common across many Muslim cultures. For example, Muslims generally consider it disrespectful to put the Quran on the ground. Also, language can be a very important aspect of culture, with use of the word "Allah" (Arabic for "God") cherished by Muslims, sometimes to controversial effect.[25]

So far this chapter has focused on what is in common. However, many aspects of culture and practice vary from Muslim to Muslim, or Muslim group to Muslim group. For example, although most Muslims approve of modesty in dress, there are different views among Muslims in the West concerning whether Muslim women should cover their head, and if so, how. Shown below are three different kinds of head covering, the *burqa*, the *hijab*, and the *niqab* (in that order).[26]

A woman wearing a burqa or chadri.

A woman wearing a hijab.

A woman wearing a niqab.

postures and ritual washing regimes are favoured
........uslims. For example, the particular number of prayer
..... the manner of raising hands or bowing varies. Although
......an is a popular festival, ways of celebrating it vary. Some
.slims see music as an important expression of faith, others do not.
So, as with other maps, it is vital for you to ask your Muslim friends
what is important for them.

Some things can also be culturally non-Western, without
necessarily being religious or distinctively Islamic. The headscarf is
a case in point, as shown by recent debates over head coverings in the
UK, Belgium, France and elsewhere. Many Christian women in the
Middle East and in Pakistan wear the headscarf, and for many Muslims
the choice to wear a headscarf is more cultural than religious.[27] Other
examples include the caste system, part of the cultural mindset of
some Indian Muslims in the West.

In summary, culture and practice are extremely important
elements of Islam. The more you make attempts to learn someone's
language or try someone's food, the better your friendship will be
with them. This is because you are demonstrating by your actions that
you accept them. Also, ask your Muslim friends about their practices.
As before, I have found that they are happy to respond.

*Everyone is multifaceted. What Muslims do is just one side of who
they are.*

Chapter 5

Politics and justice

One of the things that I have found Muslims love about Islam is its all-encompassing nature, which includes issues of politics and justice. There is much in common on these topics among Western Muslims, who for example generally dislike US and UK policy in the Middle East. Also, the large majority of Western Muslims feel that their government discriminates against them in some way, even across countries with widely varying immigration and settlement policies such as France, the UK and the USA. Unsurprisingly this can colour the political outlook of those feeling the discrimination. Most Muslims also say they want legal systems in the West to reflect Islamic codes to a greater extent than is currently the case.

However, even in respect of the above, consensus among Western Muslim communities does not stretch very far. In relation to foreign policy disputes, few agree on the specifics of the solution. According to *Muslim Americans* (an influential Pew Forum report published in 2007), some Muslims also have diverse views about domestic politics. This is evident in relation to the size and scope of government, whether government aid should be given to the poor, how government should relate to the legal system (for example in protecting morality in society), whether mosques should express political views, and many other issues.[28] Add to this the fact of changing views over time: in the year 2000, most American Muslims voted for George W. Bush, whereas in 2004, most voted against him.[29] In the UK, some Muslims have pushed for the inclusion on the statute books of specific religious hatred protection for Muslims. For many advocating the change, this has become extremely important, more so than other aspects of human rights, however defined.

Other questions on which Muslims profoundly differ from each other include: Should I be engaged in the political system and should I vote?[30] Which unified body should represent me?[31] Should we have the immediate imposition of *shari'a* now?[32] Can I marry a non-Muslim?[33] Now try putting yourself in the shoes of a Muslim who lives or works close to you. Consider how politics and/or the legal system may negatively impact them. It makes a massive difference whether a given Muslim is most concerned with discrimination (real or felt), a foreign policy "mistake", profiling or lack of opportunities in the workplace. Whatever the perceived political or judicial injustice, such issues might also be all-encompassing for your Muslim friend, more than any theological or cultural questions, and something that stops him or her really engaging meaningfully with any other topics. Perhaps as a result of the breadth and importance of such issues, the contest for political and other forms of leadership within Muslim communities is massive and often passionately felt. Overall, in common with other maps, this one highlights some things that are shared and some things that are disputed among Muslims.

This chapter ends with two examples of how you can show you are interested in your Muslim friend's views on politics and justice. First, in Europe there is fervent discussion in the media, politics, and academia about how to respond to the growing presence of Muslim minorities, how to address "the Islamist threat", and how to preserve (if this is the right thing to do) a sense of national, or European, identity.[34] Muslim views on politics and justice are being formed in the context of these kinds of discussions, which are happening around them and over which they often feel they have little control. This is a tonic against thinking that Muslim views on politics and justice in the West are created in a vacuum. The more you are aware of the importance of questions of minority and identity to Muslim communities, the better connection you will be able to make with them. In this area perhaps more than most, try to ask questions about issues of politics and justice in as even-handed a way as possible. These are topics that often inflame the passions. Ask your Muslim friend in what way they think of national or regional politics and how they think it impacts them. Or ask some specific questions, such as whether they believe Turkey should become a full member of the European Union.

Second, several commentators have noted a trend towards the re-Islamization of British Muslim youth, referring to the fact that many second- and third-generation young Muslims are more theologically devout and politically motivated than their parents.[35] To the extent that this is true, it is sowing important seeds of change in the make-up of Islam for the future. Muslims in the West may be becoming much more politically engaged. So ask your Muslim friend how their expression of Islam differs from that of their parents. By showing awareness of and interest in what for many are the most important and emotive issues in the world, you will build important relational bridges.

Everyone is multifaceted. Muslims' political views are just one facet of who they are.

Chapter 6

Demographics

Demographics involves statistics. I am aware that the mere mention of the word "statistics" brings some people out in a cold sweat. If so, this chapter may be a little harder going for you than the other chapters. But take heart: I have tried to keep it simple so that you can get a good overview – it will help you understand the context in which your Muslim friends operate.

Let's start with the overall picture. Roughly one in four people on the planet is Muslim. That is more than 1.5 billion people, counting young children whose identity cards show them as being Muslim by virtue of their parents' Islamic identity.[36] As the table opposite indicates, in just a few Western countries there are around twenty-five million Muslims, widely distributed.

Why are these figures important? Wherever you live in the West, there are likely to be Muslims near you, studying in or otherwise influencing the place where you live. Also, the Muslims living near you will probably be very aware that they live as a minority, a fact that could have an impact on their political outlook as well as other ways they see the world. Be sensitive to the fact that those you are speaking to may feel outnumbered. This feeling will be stronger in some places than others. For example, in some parts of the USA tensions over terrorism linked to the Taliban and al-Qaeda remain high and Muslims are in a small minority. These two things combined understandably lead to some Muslims feeling victimized and/or reluctant to engage with others. Finally, a point that is often overlooked in discussions about Islam in Europe is that there are at least as many Muslims living in Eastern and Central Europe as in the rest of Europe.

Number of Muslims in selected Western regions (approx.)[37]

Countries/regions	Numbers of Muslims (millions)
North America	
USA[38]	2
Canada	0.7
Europe[39]	
Balkans (Albania, Kosovo, Bosnia-Herzegovina, Bulgaria, and the Republic of Macedonia)	7.5
Germany	4
Netherlands	1
France	3.5
UK	2
Rest of Europe	4
Selected others	
South Africa	0.7
Australia	0.35

Now, let's dive a bit deeper. In Europe, immigration has historically tended to swell the number and proportion of Muslims. Also, the average birth rate of a Muslim woman in Europe has been around three times that of a non-Muslim woman in Europe. If this continues, the number of Muslims in Europe will continue to rise, in terms of both the quantity of Muslims and their proportion of the overall European population. However, it is also possible that economic factors and increasing Westernization will combine to reduce the gap in birth rates. Linear growth rate predictions for the European Muslim population should therefore be taken with a pinch of salt, along with assumptions that Muslims will soon be in the majority in the West. Nevertheless, the historic rapid rate of growth brings its own challenges and opportunities. Many Muslims living near you may be new to the country or recently have new additions to their families, something which forms an important part of their stories.

What about demographic issues other than size and growth of population? Compared with the general US population, the adult Muslim population in the USA is on average younger and less likely to own a house.[40] Overall, Muslims in the USA and Europe have lower incomes than the general populations in which they live, although the disparity is larger in Europe.[41] One report in the UK also found that on average Muslims are more likely than non-Muslims in the UK to be in poverty and/or to be in prison.[42]

Now, the above information is helpful and, in my experience, some kitchen-table discussions and much media commentary alike could often do with a more solid grounding in facts such as those above. However, helpful though generalizations are as far as they go, they also mask wide divergences. Consider the following which relates to the UK and illustrates a wider point. According to the 2001 Census, in Tower Hamlets in London 36.4 per cent of respondents were Muslims, whereas in the Isles of Scilly the percentage was zero according to the local authority. This sort of variety is also apparent in relation to social mobility, wealth and other demographic indicators or Muslims in the West. So when you meet a Muslim, don't let demographic generalizations colour your thinking too much.

I remember once having a conversation in English with a Greek person and being told, confidently, that my accent was Australian. (No offence to my Aussie friends, but my accent most certainly is not Australian.) To that Greek it made no difference. To me the difference was huge. In the same way, it is vital to be aware of the variety of nations represented by Muslims in your country and in your neighbourhood. Only 35 per cent of Muslims in the USA were born there, even though more than three-quarters of Muslims in the USA are American citizens. Many Muslims in America hail from South Asia and Iran, and only 24 per cent were born in Arab regions of the Middle East or North Africa.[43] In the UK, nearly three-quarters of those identifying as Muslims in the 2001 Census were of Bangladeshi,

Indian, Pakistani, or other Asian origin, with the vast majority of those being first- to third-generation immigrants.[44] This non-Arab bias is reflected in continental Europe, where for example the large numbers of Muslims living in Eastern Europe include significant numbers of indigenous Muslims, as well as many non-Arab (and some Arab) Muslims. So don't make the mistake of assuming, as some do, that all Muslims are Arabs. Challenge stereotypes through a mindset of genuine interest and respect.

Be interested in where other people are from, how they live, and where they live. As with every map in this section, do not treat this just as information to be gained but as an opportunity to get to know people.

Everyone is multifaceted. Where Muslims are from is just one aspect of who they are.

Chapter 7

Before folding the maps away...

One thing this whirlwind tour has shown us is how small an amount of terrain we have really covered, relative to Islam as a whole. Google Maps and Streetview now allow us to zoom right in, even to the level of seeing past the pink curtains of your front room (as some have discovered to their embarrassment). However, even though we have not gone quite that far in this chapter, we have zoomed in some considerable way. My hope is that the journey we have taken will help us guard against reducing Islam to any one factor. The background or opinions of whatever Muslims we happen to have met understandably colour our view of Muslims generally. Add to that the bias of whatever books, newspapers, TV channels, or websites we get our ideas about Muslims from, and it is inevitable that we all have a partial view of who Muslims are. So, as we proceed, you will do well to keep in mind the variety and depth of maps that exist (and there are others besides those I have illustrated).

Muslims are diverse. So what? Returning to the map analogy, even if you had extensive knowledge of all the maps of Oxford (even stretching to knowledge of the "Inspector Morse Location Map of Oxford"), your understanding of Oxford would be woefully inadequate.[45] To rectify this, you would need to speak with those who live there or have lived there, those who really know the place. In fact, if it were a choice between studying maps and getting to know people, you would probably learn more about the real Oxford if you got to know the people. Even when it comes to getting from A to B, a quick conversation with a taxi driver or cyclist may be more helpful than buying a road map. Similarly, to understand Islam and Muslims, get to know Muslims yourself. Of course, the maps have their uses, so don't ignore them completely. But allow the diversity of Muslims to be a delightful excuse (if you need one) to get to know those Muslims around you even better.

Part 2

Developing open-hearted friendships: Tips for connecting with Muslims

The aim of this section is to inspire you to build open-hearted friendships with Muslims. This involves having the right mindset and putting that mindset into action. So Chapters 10–13 (the core of this section) focus on how we can welcome, accept and be honest with Muslims, not just in how we think but also in what we do.

Of course, much of this section is applicable to anybody, not just Muslims. So you will find that much of the advice and many of the tools that follow are more widely applicable than just in relation to Islam.

One final point before we proceed. The more you get to know Muslims, the more important it is to be clear on how your witness to Muslims connects with the strategic vision and direction of your local church. (Appendix 4 deals with this issue from a leadership perspective.) If you have a heart to reach Muslims and this is not shared by your leaders, make sure you proceed wisely. By all means witness to your friends, but don't try in a behind-the-scenes way to sway the direction of the church as if you were a leader. Rather, as appropriate, arrange to meet with your leaders. Once you have agreed a clear way forward, stick to it.

Chapter 8

Why focus on open-hearted friendships?

There is a debate – often very impassioned – that has been running in Christian circles for several years now about how best to reach Muslims. To illustrate the spectrum of views, let me characterize the two extremes of this debate (with the extreme of the extremes in brackets):

- Confrontation – sometimes called the polemic approach. Those taking this approach generally feel comfortable when debating. They are robust in the way they point to the superiority of Christianity, even where this involves a comparison with Islam and critiquing it. For example, they may challenge the credibility of the Quran (even if the manner of the challenge personally offends Muslims, with the offence not really being due to "the stumbling block of the cross").

- Peace – sometimes called the irenic approach. Those taking this approach emphasize what is shared, such as "desire for God" or "giving financially to the poor", and might downplay differences in beliefs (even hiding distinctive beliefs).

A nagging unease has remained with me as I have observed this debate, which has occasionally spilled over into questioning the Christian commitment of those involved. Here I am not talking about what is in brackets above – the extremes of the extremes, which I think are very unhelpful. In relation to the rest of it, I can understand why particular personality types or experience may influence some to a more confrontational or peaceful approach. Each approach has drawbacks and strengths: for example, challenging a worldview may help remove a set of ear-muffs that is preventing your friend from really hearing you, or avoiding confrontation may help keep the conversation going longer. But my unease stems from an impression that we needn't choose between the approaches. The more I reflected on the nature of friendship, the stronger this impression became.

Although it is a virtue to be consistent, surely it is also in the very nature of friendship to act in different ways with the same friend at different times. Think about Jesus and Judas: did not Jesus both wash his feet and rebuke and confront him (John 13)? So, where my friend has done something wrong, I might confront him or her. Where my friend has pointed out a fault of mine, I might apologize, remembering the first part of Proverbs 27:6, *"Wounds from a friend can be trusted."* Where a misunderstanding has occurred, real friends assume the best. Peacefully and gently, they try to understand why the other person acted in that way. In the case of Muslims, you will not need to choose between a confrontational and a peaceful approach where real open-hearted friendship is your paradigm. For example, you will want to emphasize acts of mercy that are shared, such as helping rebuild the homes of earthquake survivors in Pakistan (acts that many Muslims are involved in) as well as, at the right time, confronting the usual Muslim understanding that Jesus is neither God the Son nor Saviour. There is no contradiction in the types of approach involved here. Friends both confront and seek peace. In short, they are loving. Of course, it is also open-hearted friendship that is most likely to yield the real questions, the questions of the heart.

Think about other episodes Jesus was involved in. The way he went about his public ministry was with twelve close followers – friends – who were with him regularly. On many occasions, Jesus chose to go out of his way to spend considerable amounts of time with people, such as with Zacchaeus in Luke 19. These decisions must have enhanced the possibility of open-hearted friendships. Alongside this, when faced by those bent on confronting him Jesus met them firmly. Examples include interactions with the rich young ruler (Matthew 19:16–22), the Pharisees and Herodians (Mark 12:13–17), a Pharisee at a dinner party (Luke 7:36–50), and Pharisees who had come to challenge him (Matthew 23:13–36). So although friendship was important to Jesus, this man of peace did not understand his interactions with others in a way that excluded the possibility of confrontation.[46]

The approach of the apostle Paul underlines this. He was able to confront and be irenic and did not appear to choose between the extremes I have characterized above.[47]

Are you the type of person who shies away from any confrontation? Remember that love is sometimes gentle and sometimes tough. As a loving father or friend does, we must discern which approach is best at any given time. In the context of a rising influence of extremist fundamentalism among Muslims in the West, I would go further. It may sometimes be appropriate to confront the views of a Muslim whom we have just met. However, there is a world of difference between on the one hand attacking Islam because of fear and being uninformed and, on the other, confronting real issues in a settled, calm way at the right time. In the former case, we are captive to our emotions. In the latter, we are flowing freely, secure on the rock of our faith, speaking always with a respectful tone and in ways that honour the other.

Or are you the type of person who is always spoiling for a fight? Remember that confrontation is more effective when it takes place in the context of a trusting friendship. Within a friendship the questions are much less likely to be smokescreens for the real issues. Also, if you "press pause" on certain discussions, they can much more easily be followed up later.

In summary, aim to inspire open-hearted friendships and avoid the "extremes of the extremes" of personal offence and hiding differences. It is deep friendships that will provide the soil from which fruitful interactions are most likely to grow.

Chapter 9

Addressing the fear factor

"The anticipation of rejection is often worse than the actual experience."[48]

The story is told of a man who decided it was time for a promotion and salary increase at work.He bolstered his courage, scheduled an appointment with his boss, and began to prepare his argument. Anticipating refusal, he built his case like a barrister in a capital case defending the life of an innocent man. *When I walk into his office*, the worker thought, *I will put my arguments to him and demand my rise. When he turns me down, I will say, "I've poured my life into building this company for twenty years." And when he refuses to accept my proposal, I will respond, "Either you give me a rise or I resign!" And when he stares defiantly at me, I will storm out of the office and never return.* After considering what he was up against, the man simply boxed up his personal belongings and left the office without even going to speak to his boss. His anticipation of a turndown had left him paralysed with fear. [49]

Fear can be a big reason why some Christians do not develop meaningful relationships with many non-Christians, including Muslims. The following statements illustrate what is often going on beneath the surface:

Quran? Muhammad? Hadith? My lack of knowledge will be exposed, and I'll be outgunned in conversation.

Most Muslims I know dress differently to me, speak a different language and eat different foods. I fear looking silly if I engage with them.

I don't have any Muslim friends, and they wouldn't want to be my friend anyway.

I desire all to come to know Jesus, but what if I'm not fruitful enough?

The media tell me that Muslims sympathize with terrorism. I'm afraid of meeting someone like that.

Discuss Bible history? Explain the Trinity? Give me a break – I couldn't do that!

An important aspect of addressing fear is to recognize that it is there.

Part of the reason why many Christians are afraid to develop relationships with Muslims is also that they do not understand how secure and privileged their own personal relationship with Jesus Christ is. If you have fears related to this that you know are deep-seated, can I encourage you in the first instance to talk and pray about this with a Christian leader that you trust? For all of us, the better rooted we are in Jesus, the more confident we will be that the Holy Spirit will work in the lives of our friends, and the better foundations we are laying for effective mission to Muslims. Be proactive and intentional about addressing deep-seated fears of the kind that prevent you really opening up with non-Christians.

Also, through his Holy Spirit God is at work among Muslims worldwide. Many Muslims around the world report experiences of Jesus in response to asking for revelation from God, and many have also come to follow Jesus. So much has been documented about this that reading and watching it would keep you occupied for months. Here are some sources where you can find Muslims telling their own stories of how Jesus showed himself to them and of how they came to follow Jesus, from a variety of perspectives:

- www.morethandreams.org – docudrama testimonies of how Christ met Muslims through dreams and visions: the stories of Khalil (a radical Egyptian terrorist), Mohammad (a Fulani herdsman in Nigeria), Dini (an Indonesian teenager), Khosrow (a young Iranian man), and Ali (a Turkish man addicted to alcohol).

- *I Dared to Call Him Father,* by Bilquis Sheikh, a Pakistani woman.

- www.answering-Islam.org/Testimonies/index.html – stories of Muslim men and women from Israel, Egypt, Palestine, Jordan, Iraq, Kurdistan, Kuwait, Syria, Lebanon, Kosovo, Turkey, Saudi Arabia, Iran, Russia, Pakistan, India, Afghanistan, Morocco, Algeria, Nigeria, Somalia, Indonesia, Malaysia, Trinidad, the UK, the USA, and elsewhere.[50]

These things are happening today. We need not fear lack of response or interest!

Crucially, many of the above stories involve friendships with Christians, and friendship is not something to fear. It is my conviction that the single best thing you can do to reach Muslims is to try to *build open-hearted friendships with them*. This approach is effective, simple, and fun. Hopefully, the preceding chapters of this book will have given you a greater understanding of the cultural, theological, and other underpinnings of Islam, as well as inspiration for reaching out to Muslims. But knowledge and inspiration like this alone are not enough. The central practical application of this book is to help you develop open-hearted friendships with Muslims, so it is to this that we now turn.

Chapter 10

Cultivate a posture of welcome and acceptance

How confident are you that if ten Muslims were given privileged access to your life, they would be fascinated by the Christ-like nature of *who you are*?

One of the things I love most about Jesus is the desire he showed to cross racial and other barriers of mistrust, such as with the Samaritan woman in John 4. To what extent do you really welcome and accept those who are different from you? In some ways, this chapter is different from the two that follow. Whereas speaking and acting are largely about *doing*, this chapter is about *being*. What is your mindset towards Muslims?

To be most authentic as a follower of Jesus, and to lay a foundation for developing open-hearted friendships with Muslims, we must primarily have a posture of welcome and acceptance towards Muslims. Two practical suggestions for achieving this posture follow:

1. Pray for open hearts

What should we pray for in respect of Islam, both in our private prayer and in our church prayer meetings? For an increase in the number of followers of Jesus across the whole Islamic world? For churches to spring up in that same region? For mosque attenders, *shari'a* court judges, and halal butchers in our nations to be impacted by the gospel in all its multifaceted beauty? For me to have my first conversation with a Muslim? Yes, yes, yes, and yes. These are good things to pray for, so pray for them. God is able to do much more than you ask or imagine. In addition, pray for the kind of things the apostle Paul prayed for – boldness, clarity, and open doors.

Yet also I have found one thing to be most releasing and effective in this area: pray for open hearts. Pray that your own heart would be open to what God is doing among Muslims. Pray for connections with Muslims whose hearts are open to you and to Jesus. In your devotions, ask God, "Which Muslims around me are genuinely open to finding out more about Jesus?" In your prayer meetings, pray for favour when you name Jesus in relevant contexts. In my experience, as God answers such prayers, relationships open up and I have then felt less pressure, being more aware of God's sovereign work in others. I have also found that this way my own stance becomes more welcoming and accepting towards Muslims.

As you pray in this way, you will find that you and others become more motivated to reach out to Muslims.

You may also want to pray in particular during the month of Ramadan, the ninth month in the Islamic lunar calendar (the "Hijri calendar").[51] During the Night of Power (this is usually one of the last two or three nights of Ramadan for Muslims of Pakistani and Bangladeshi origin), Muslims pray that God would reveal himself to them, and Jesus often does!

2. Be interested in others

Don't know whether to offer a Muslim a beer? Don't know your Sufi from your Sunni? Just ask your Muslim friend. It shows that you are interested and that you value his or her opinion. Perhaps he or she will reciprocate, but even if not, you will be closer than before as friends. Have a mindset of being interested in others.

Along with this goes openness about ourselves. Let me encourage you not to trudge through daily life, head down, in your own private cocoon. Do all you can to raise your sights and to show by your interest that you welcome and accept your Muslim friends.

To illustrate this, imagine the following fictional scenario.[52] On your bus journey to work over the last few months, you have got to know Ahmed, a retired Bangladeshi Muslim who migrated to the UK and moved into the area in 1951. His wife Fatima is his first cousin, and they met in their teens in their village outside Dhaka. They have three married sons, all in their late thirties or early forties: Mahmood and Mustafa manage their own restaurants; Muhammad is the "black sheep" of the family, being a heavy drinker and never having held down a job for more than a month. (To help him out, Mahmood sometimes employs him in his restaurant.) Mahmood has four children, two at secondary school, one at primary school, and one in nursery. Ahmed and Fatima also have two daughters, one of whom is Hawwa, aged twenty-one, extremely bright and the first member of the family to study at university. Are you curious enough to find out these kind of things? Or don't you care? With the exception of how Muhammad is viewed by his family, all of the above information is the kind of thing that most such families would be happy to share. Are you curious enough to find out even more? This does not make you nosey, just a potentially good friend.

Chapter 11

Show by your actions that you welcome and accept Muslims

"As we seek to confront Muslims with Jesus Christ, we must rely upon the dynamic fascination of radiant, Christlike living. This… is more subtle than reasoned argument, more persuasive than an educational enterprise, and more effective than any amount of formal religious instruction."[53]

1. Actually get to know some Muslims

It may sound over-simple, but a great piece of advice is simply to take the plunge. Get to know some Muslims. Don't be personally distant from those Muslims around you. Whether at a café bar, at a community centre or in the shops, take opportunities to get to know them. Jesus was not so consumed with meeting his followers that he had no time for others. As much as possible, try to get to know Muslims of the same gender as you.

Here are a couple of ideas. Go round to your Muslim neighbour and say "Eid Mubarak" (which roughly means "Happy Eid") at the time of one of the two Eids. Take cake. Get invited in. Have a wonderful time. (In many Western "my-home-is-my-castle" societies, people can resent having someone knock on their door seemingly randomly. But in many non-Western cultures, one way to honour people is to go to their house, knock on the door and receive hospitality from them.) Another idea is to hold a huge party at New Year, perhaps choosing New Year according to the calendar of those you're inviting.[54]

**How not to put your foot in it in
the first thirty seconds when meeting a Muslim**

1. Greet them.

2. If they offer you food, eat what is put before you.

3. If you're carrying a Bible or other holy book, do not put it on the floor.

4. Ask them about their family and country of origin.

5. If their first language is not English, ask them to teach you how to say "Hello" in their language.

6. When you put your foot in it, don't be above laughing at yourself and apologizing.

2. Show love in action

"Our problem in evangelism is not a lack of training. The problem is that we don't love enough. Do you need training to talk to your grandchildren?"[55]

Imagine it is Sunday at 1 p.m. Your church meeting ended half an hour ago and you notice Ahmed and Salima, two Jordanian Muslims interested in finding out more about Jesus. They are about to leave. The worst thing you can do is walk over, greet them warmly, and say, "See you next Sunday!" I exaggerate slightly. There probably are worse things you could do. But my point is this: Middle Eastern ideas of community do not involve a two-hour fix once a week. (Neither do those of most of the rest of the world.) This caricature is the basis for the Muslim response, "Islam is a 24-7 religion, as opposed to the once-a-week-on-a-Sunday religion of Western Christianity."

Think hard about the extent to which your church is community at all times, not just on Sunday mornings. How are you showing Muslims that you love them during the week? This is vital if you are to bridge the cultural and practical gaps highlighted in Part 1. Yes, individual evangelism is important, but we can't treat Muslims just as individuals; they are part of families and communities.

Many of us in the West also need to get better at interacting with those from non-Western nations (to say nothing of Muslims). By "better" I mean more loving, which includes being sensitive, welcoming, open, and honest. If there are some people near you who are already modelling this very well, learn from them. Finally, it is important to think about how Muslims will respond to being invited to Christian religious gatherings such as church or community groups. What aspects of how such gatherings work might be barriers to Muslim enquirers?

There are no simple formulas here. Perhaps you will end up with more shared meals, open homes, or practical help for new parents. Whether the ideas involve big programmes is not the point. Pray, seek, and plan along these lines, and the right ideas will emerge.

3. Get engaged in politics and issues of social need

Consider getting involved in some kind of social, political, and/or educational action, for example with initiatives that Muslims will readily support. Here are some ideas about how you can get to know Muslims while being involved in wider society:

- Become a governor at a local school where there are Muslims.
- Put on a course teaching English as a foreign language.
- Run a group or course for women and provide child care. (Make sure all the teachers are women.)
- Volunteer at an asylum welcome centre. (Or develop expertise in relation to asylum cases and set up a housing scheme for failed asylum seekers. This is much more ambitious, not to be entered into lightly.)

Some Muslims are pushing hard for distinctively Islamic elements to be included in educational syllabuses. Other Muslims want to build mosques. Is it your inclination to oppose such things? I would recommend caution in respect of the following. Some anti-mosque campaigns are against the principle of religious freedom that it is important for Christians to uphold. And a negative approach can sometimes hinder the building of open-hearted friendships.

But what about issues relevant to politics and society on which some Muslims and Christians would take different sides? For example, there are *shari'a* courts in the UK that advocate inferior divorce rights for women as compared with men. Should such courts be allowed wider influence? You may want to work on such issues, for example by getting involved in local politics or think-tanks.

Overall, beware of getting so obsessed with political engagement that you forgo other ways of interacting with Muslims (or interacting with others about Islam). In some quarters in the West, Christians have become so besotted with some single issue (such as a local mosque or school) that it seriously detracts from our overall message. Certainly, there are occasions when a seemingly inconsequential decision can set a precedent and act as a bridgehead for a significant increase in influence later on. But when the only thing policy makers hear from Christians is "Muslim influence on legal issues is dangerous" or "Resist Muslim sway over education", they may get the impression that we have little that is positive or nuanced to say. Be sure to reflect and communicate the glorious breadth of what the church has to offer to politics, society, and issues of justice.

Also beware of stoking fear and mistrust. The main sources of information about Islam for some Christians are media and press outlets that emphasize the negative effects of Islam on our tax burden (for example via immigration) and on our security (for example via the threat of religious extremism). These sources frequently obscure the joy of meeting Muslims, and their rich, multifaceted, cultural and ethnic heritages. Excessive focus on purely political engagement may play to prejudices that can be unhelpful in the extreme.

Chapter 12

Level with your Muslim friends

Part of good friendship is being open and honest about what you believe. As you get to know Muslims, do not try to water down your own faith perspective, as if a lowest common denominator approach may somehow gain favour and develop friendship. This chapter focuses on aspects of being open and honest about what we believe.

1. Invite others into The Story and your story

Consider the following way of telling a parable to a Muslim. "Two men… went to the mosque to pray at the call to prayer. The first man performed all the ablutions and ceremonial requirements but had his mind not on God but on the beautiful girl in the next house. The second man was so overcome by shame for his sins that he left out the ablutions and ceremonial requirements, and cried out to God for mercy." A Muslim hearing this story and asked to say which man he thought God would more readily accept, will often say that the first man gained God's favour, for he fulfilled the ritual.[56]

Instead of telling a story like the one above, imagine if you had started by saying, "I'm going to read you a story from the Bible," and had read Luke 18:9–14. Some people will be open to this approach. But many Muslims may feel cornered and turn to defences such as, "But the Bible has been changed." By first making contact, engagingly and in a non-threatening way, with somebody's worldview, you may be much better placed to invite them into the worldview that has so captivated you. For example, after telling the above parable, try asking, "Would you like to hear a story about how Jesus responded in a similar situation?" This way, the biblical story may get a more engaged hearing.[57]

Be encouraged that many Muslims view the Bible fundamentally positively. At one meeting I attended, a Muslim from Saudi Arabia said the following while holding a Bible, "This is a holy book. We must not just read it and put it in our hearts, but we must put it into action in our lives." These are wonderful words. Many Muslims also view the possibility of God's involvement in physical healing positively. These are open doors for us to share stories of God's work through history and in our lives.

Think about how you can get really good at storytelling. This includes biblical stories and stories of your own experiences of getting to know God. Tell stories of love poured out, of healing, of great escapes, and tell them in compelling ways. This will help create open doors with Muslims, since their cultural heritage is often so very story-centric.

2. Prepare to give answers

Some Muslims have significant doctrinal questions about Christianity. As you get ready to address them, you may be glad to know that it is easier than you think. Muslims do not generally expect Christians to be experts in Islam, but Muslims do expect Christians to know something about Christianity. The questions that come up about Christianity usually relate to the contents and history of the Bible and the nature of God (for example the Trinity, and/or who Jesus is). So your preparation to give answers should start by focusing on these areas. If you are likely to be challenged about the Bible, is it not important to know your way around it? Do not just learn parts of it by rote; learn also to reason from the Bible. To what extent can you really justify your own beliefs from the Bible, rather than just repeat confessional doctrine?

When you are asked to give a reason for the faith you hold, do not shy away from this opportunity. Lots of moderate Muslims are rejecting extremism but want to believe in God. The door is opening for us to give to such Muslims reasons for the hope we have. Open-hearted friendship is consistent with direct gospel challenge. After all, the more trusting (i.e. the stronger) the bridge of friendship, the more theological load it will be able to bear.

It is also important to be alert to where questions are really coming from. The nature of the biblical challenge put by many Muslims is different to what many of us have faced in the past. Traditional secular and/or atheist polemicists may claim that certain scriptures do not stand up to rational scrutiny, whereas Muslims are more likely to find it incredible that God could let man corrupt his Word, as Muslim apologists put it.

Addressing an objection to trusting today's Old and New Testaments

The Quran refers positively to "the Scripture before", meaning "the Scripture before the Quran", and names the Torah, Psalms and Gospels. These are integral parts of the Bible available today. But a common objection to Christianity among Muslims is to allege that "the Scripture before" has been changed and corrupted and is therefore unreliable. If faced with this objection, it is helpful to ask several questions.

Where does it say that in the Quran? Some Muslims point to *Sura* 2:79 which says, "Then woe to those who write the Book with their own hands, and then say: 'This is from Allah,' to traffic with it for miserable price! Woe to them for what their hands do write, and for the gain they make thereby." Or to *Sura* 3:78: "There is among them a section who distort the Book with their tongues..." But these verses are far from clear in establishing the above objection. Another verse in the Quran that refers to a holy book being declared false or cut into parts refers to the Quran itself (*Sura* 15:91). That is, the Quran does not seem to make the above objection.[58]

If you are faced with the above objection, also try asking: When are you claiming that (part of) the Bible was corrupted? Before or after the revelation of the Quran?

If before, then what of *Sura* 6:114–5? Here, Allah effectively affirms to Muhammad that he gave the Scripture, that it is perfect and that no one can change it. These verses refer to the Scripture before the Quran. Is the Quran therefore misleading in stating that no one can change the word of Allah?

If after (that is, if "the Scripture before" has been corrupted or changed at some time between the time of Muhammad and the present day), then (the objection goes) surely that would mean that we cannot trust today's Bible. In response, two points can be made. First, if we restrict ourselves to a translation of the Gospels solely based on manuscripts dating from before the time of Muhammad, apart from two well-known twelve verse sections[59], all such manuscripts contain the same stories in the same sequence. Second, why is it that many of the early Muslim writers studied and appreciated the Bible (Old and New Testaments) and regarded it as inspired? For example, the Muslim commentator on the Quran al-Tabari (who died in AD 923) may be counted among this number, and he quoted the Bible frequently. There are no documented instances in Muslim pre-modern sources of the Bible being definitively changed after the time of al-Tabari. That is, evidence both internal and external to the Muslim tradition argues against the possibility that "the Scripture before" was changed after the time of Muhammad.

Chapter 13

Keep welcoming Muslims as they come to follow Jesus

Migrating[60]

Imagine you have to migrate to another country. What challenges will you face? You will have to learn a new language, find a new circle of friends, and work out what are your new culture's unwritten codes of conduct. How will you fit in? How long will it take to feel at home? And meanwhile you are mourning the loss of all you left behind. It's a massive dislocation.

Migrating to a new religion can be as difficult as migrating to a new country. We don't realize this in our individualistic Western society, where "conversion" seems mostly to be a matter of changing our personal beliefs. But in the rest of the world (and to some extent among ethnic minorities in the West) collectivist cultures are the norm. Your religion is not your private affair, but part of your group identity. Therefore to migrate to another faith is to dishonour your family and betray your tribe. "Don't you realize," a former Muslim friend of ours was told by her relative, "that by becoming a Christian you have abandoned your roots, your heritage, and your family name?" For many Muslims, the real challenge is not just turning to Christ but growing strong in him afterwards, serving him actively, and joining the fellowship of his people.

When Muslims you know are ready to become followers of Jesus, are you ready? Do you have the right resources (e.g. bilingual Bibles or simple prayer response cards) around you or in your church? What thought have you put into addressing (long-term) family and community implications for those showing interest in Christ, of the kind alluded to in the above quotation?

We are aiming for disciples – not just individuals, but families and communities. Discipling Muslims who have decided to follow Jesus is a vital task, as the following quotes from believers from a Muslim background indicate.[61]

"It seems that churches expect new believers to adapt to [their] Western-style set-up and have very little understanding of the cost and suffering of converts from Islam or of their responsibility to them to be their new family."

"Post-baptism was a crucial time for me, but no one from church was there to walk through the wilderness with me. As a newcomer I felt isolated – I felt very lonely."

"I became integrated straightaway, but it was a further ten years before I realized I had lost my cultural identity."

To neglect the task of discipleship is to abdicate our responsibility as friends.

As with the discipleship of any new believer, there is no simple formula, but the few tips that follow are important to bear in mind. Recall the earlier story of a Muslim leaving church and being told, "See you next Sunday" – the very antithesis of community in the minds of many non-Westerners? Help believers from Muslim backgrounds to be engaged with Christian communities around you. The strength of the *umma* (the global Muslim community of believers) makes this even more important. Many Western Muslims are used to daily connections through after-school clubs, language schools and the like. It is important that we offer believers from Muslim backgrounds connections that will also help their spiritual development. Be available to them when they need you, not just at prearranged times.

As early as reasonable, address cross-cultural sensitivities that come up, such as about food, forms of dress, relating to family, and so on. As part of this, help new believers to be discerning in terms of whether any given sensitivity has to do with the gospel. (See the box below as well as Chapter 27, "Is it OK for Christians to eat halal meat?")

The question of when a new believer should tell his or her natural family about their conversion is very important. If you are discipling new believers in this situation, offer to help them think through how and when to raise the topic. Many former Muslims express regret at the hasty and naïve way in which they told their parents and siblings about their conversion. Rejection is unfortunately a real possibility. (One study of sixteen Muslims in the UK who began to follow Jesus found that in every case but one, the reaction of their families was negative, with isolation, bribery, imprisonment and hitting among the threats or punishments meted out.[62]) However, some considerate advanced planning can have a positive bearing on how well the initial conversations with families go.

But it's also true that missionaries (and indeed the national Christian community) have often made matters worse by extracting Muslim background believers too quickly from their own society and culture. I have even heard of Muslim background belivers being asked to prove the genuineness of their faith by eating pork! They are expected not only to turn to Christ but also to adopt so-called "Christian"customs or wear "Christian'"clothes (whatever those are). No wonder this causes unnecessary offence.[63]

Finally, of course, everyone in a church should ideally be welcoming and everyone should help integrate others into the church, to the extent those others want to be integrated. But bearing in mind the work involved (and, in some cases, the specialist knowledge), it can be helpful to have some people who are dedicated to the task of helping those of Muslim background begin journeying with Christ and integrate into the church.

Part 3

Seeing Jesus afresh:
Outlines to help Muslims

I love the National Gallery in London. One of my favourite paintings there is *The Ambassadors*, a 1533 work by Hans Holbein the Younger. By the time I reached my mid-twenties I must have seen it at least five times. This was a painting I thought I knew well. One day in 2001, I had a spare half-hour and happened to be near Trafalgar Square. So I popped into the National Gallery and found that a short lunchtime talk was about to start. The location and topic of the talk? You've guessed it: *The Ambassadors*. For ten minutes I was transfixed as a blazered expert grippingly described the meticulous detail of the painting and various interpretations and meanings connected with it. (I won't spoil the fun for you by giving a half-baked summary. Go and enjoy it yourself!) That talk helped me appreciate so much more of what was there in something I thought I knew. Though it was the last thing I expected, I saw *The Ambassadors* afresh that day.

Jesus is central in the Islamic faith. According to Muslims, Jesus is a prophet who will return at the final resurrection. On almost every occasion that I have mentioned Jesus' name to a Muslim, they have responded with respect, a nod, a smile, and/or some other expression of happiness. As a Christian, I rejoice that Muslims like Jesus already. I am also eager for them to see him afresh.

This section offers a range of options – think of them as ten displays in a gallery – to help Muslims appreciate the beauty on offer in Jesus. Each outline uses one of three different starting points:

echoes of truth within Islam, the Bible, and Christmas. Not every option will appeal to everyone. Remember from Part 1 of this book that Muslims are delightfully multifaceted people. More intellectual types may be drawn to the outline that uses "Jesus as a prophet" as a starting point. If your friend has already asked you as a Christian to tell them more about Jesus, why not go straight to the Bible? But if the trustworthiness of the Bible is a big issue for your friend, don't necessarily dive straight into the Bible-based outlines. A little forethought about which approach will work best will be handsomely repaid. Also, feel free to modify the outlines according to your needs.

Finally, remember from Part 2 that the aim is to build open-hearted friendships with Muslims, not to score cheap points. In using the outlines contained in this section with your Muslim friends, think about what subsequent dialogue opportunities they may generate. Asking follow-up questions such as "What interested you most about that?" is an extremely important part of the use of this material. Enjoy!

Chapter 14

Starting from echoes of truth in Islam: Outline A – Arabia is important

This outline differs from the others in that it simply tries to remove a specific barrier to considering Christian views on anything, including Jesus. The barrier is the perception that Westerners look down on the Middle East. By contrast, we should recognize that Arabia is important, because it is the region where Islam started. This region, and more broadly the Middle East, contains many cities and sites of importance to Muslims.

You may want to use this outline as a conversation-starter or as part of an introduction to a talk or small group discussion.

God loves Muslims. He makes the sun shine and the rain fall on them, and loves blessing them abundantly. But in addition to this, have you noticed the importance of Arabia and its surroundings in biblical revelation?

As Christians we can affirm that this region is important.[64] For example, Israelite worship in the Temple depended on spices such as myrrh, not obtainable in Israel but found in Arabia. The Bible presents many "people of the East" (the East includes Arabia) as having close relationships with God and as being known for their wisdom. There is a long scholarly history of associating Job, and the story of Job, with Arabia and the Arabic language. For example, Elihu was from among the Buzites, who lived next to the Chaldeans in north-east Arabia. Also, Moses' father-in-law was a priest of the Lord in Arabia even before God revealed himself to Moses on Mount Sinai.

Fast-forwarding to New Testament times, we find Luke (writer of the Gospel of Luke and the book of Acts) recording with approval the fact that Arabs were declaring the wonders of God in their own language.[65] Immediately after his conversion, Saul of Tarsus (Paul) went to Arabia to adjust to his new calling from God.[66]

This is all quite important, given that Arabia is where Islam started. We might add to this the point that other parts of the world significant in the early spread of Islam are also biblically important. For example, Jesus came from what is now Palestine, and Abraham came from what is now Iraq. As Christians, if we are authentic to our roots, we love Arabia and the Middle East. It is in our DNA!

Chapter 15

Starting from echoes of truth in Islam: Outline B – Jesus is good news

There are various ways in which you could use this outline as a practical resource. You could use the material as the basis for the first part of a talk. Or if you are meeting a Muslim friend one to one, you could use it as a couple of topics of conversation. By working through the sections at your own pace, you can gauge when your friend is ready to consider other material. A question that may provide you with a way into this material is: Given the diversity of types of Muslims, how can the one Jesus be good news for them all?

Muslims already think Jesus is good news

Without Christians having to tell them, many Muslims already think that Jesus is good news. Jesus is mentioned in ninety-three *ayas* (verses) in the Quran, including the following:[67]

- "A sign" (*ayatan*, *Sura* 3:50):
  "And [I (Jesus) have come] to confirm the *Torah* that there was before me and to make lawful to you some of that which was forbidden to you. I bring you a sign from your Lord: So fear God and obey me."

- "An example" (*mathalan*, *Sura* 43:59):
  "He is only a servant on whom We bestowed blessing and We made Him an example for the Children of Israel."

- "Illustrious" or "deserving of honour" (*wajīhan*, *Sura* 3:45); also (from the same verse) "close to God" or "brought near" (*min al-muqarrabīna*) and "a word from Him" (*kalimatin minhu*)
  "And [recall] when the angels said, 'O Mary, God gives you good news of a word from Him, whose name is *al-Masīh*, Jesus, son of Mary, illustrious in this world and the next, and one of those brought near."

The Quran also gives many other honourable titles and descriptions of Jesus. It presents Jesus as a prophet (*nabī*), one of the six dignified with special titles. In Jesus' case, the prophetic title is "Spirit of God" (*rūh Allāh*). There are Muslim traditions that emphasize the sinlessness and remarkable healing ministry of Jesus.[68]

It is true that Muslim and Christian stories about Jesus differ from each other. For example, whether Jesus was crucified is a point of dispute (see Chapter 3, "Beliefs"). But we should not forget the remarkable similarities between Muslim and Christian stories about Jesus.

If wanting to know more, Muslims are authorized to ask Christians about this

So, Muslims already think Jesus is good news and honour him. Much of the information in the Quran about Jesus also invites further questions. For example:

- He was a prophet: what kind?
- He was an example: what did he come to do?
- He asked for obedience to himself: what does that mean for us?

The Quran records these important words, which address Muhammad: "If you are in doubt about what We send down to you, ask those who recited the Scripture before you. The Truth has come to you from your Lord. Do not be one of the doubters."[69]

"The Scripture before you" refers to the Pentateuch (*Tawrat*), Psalms (*Zabur*) and Gospels (*Injil*).[70] That is, if Muhammad did not want to be counted among the waverers, he should ask those who read named scriptures which are to be found in the Bible.

Although some beliefs associated with Christianity and described in the Quran differ from what was orthodox Christianity at the time,[71] this does not lessen the force for Muslims of the above Quranic material. Elsewhere, the Quran claims that "the Lord's words" cannot be changed.[72] And despite objections sometimes put forward, there are good reasons to trust the Bible we have today (see box in Chapter 12).

So, given that Christians are the ones reading "the Scripture before", and given that the Quran seems to urge those in doubt to ask such people, it is permissible for Muslims to ask Christians about Jesus. Though it may seem provocative, it is important to ask: "Has Islam paid enough attention to what is said about Jesus? Have later traditions turned Muslims away from the gospel to which the Quran refers?"[73] When asked about Jesus, you may want to turn to outlines H or I, or to point to some of the many experiences of Jesus reported by Muslims in response to asking for revelation from God (see Chapter 9).

Chapter 16

Starting from echoes of truth in Islam: Outline C – Is Jesus just a prophet?

This outline is based on a talk, "Is Jesus just a prophet?" that I was invited to give to Muslims and others at a university in the UK. This is the kind of talk you might also give if you organized a Muslim–Christian dialogue event with the local mosque to aid understanding and friendship. At such an event, one person from each faith would be allowed thirty minutes to speak and then take questions. Or you could adapt this talk to be used in a less formal setting, such as a small group discussion introduced by a fifteen-minute talk. In using this outline, make it your own by drawing on your stories as well as the material earlier in this book and in the resources section.

Introduction

When introducing yourself, include whether your family background includes any links with Islam and/or what other relevant links you may have with Islam. You may want to talk about what aspects of Islam you admire.

Today, our topic is the identity of someone about whom it seems everybody has an opinion:

- Some people think Jesus is a swear word.
- One bio-mathematician at UCLA suggests that Jesus was an alien.

- My uncle Avtar, a Hindu, thought Jesus was a great moral teacher.

- Dan Brown thinks Jesus was just a good man.

- A recent newspaper article reported that some atheists believe that Jesus was the first atheist.

  The title of today's talk is the question "Is Jesus just a prophet?" This talk addresses Islamic and Christian perspectives on this question. In the course of Islamic and Christian history various attitudes have been adopted towards Jesus. However, rather than do a historical survey, I am going back to primary sources.

Communicate the structure of your talk.

  This is a huge area and I have to be selective. As W. Cantwell Smith has said, "No statement about a religion is valid unless it can be acknowledged by that religion's believers." For those of you who are Muslims, it is my hope that what I say about Islam rings true with you.

The Quran and Jesus

Draw on some of the material in Outline B, making the points that the Quran gives Jesus a position of honour, affirms him as a prophet and as more than a prophet. Crucially, here the Quran is raising questions for us. Lead towards the question, "So, in what way is the *Injil* relevant to me?" You may wish to use the following quotation in this section:

  As in the Bible, the prophet in the Quran appears as a messenger of a particular kind, chosen for a special purpose with a message from God. The prophets brought the books of divine revelation, *Tawrat*, *Zabur* and *Injil*. Similarly, Muhammad brought "an Arabic Quran" to make the Arabs also a People of the Book. (Geoffrey Parrinder, *Jesus in the Quran*, p. 38).

Then lead towards the question, "Who should I ask to deal with these questions?" Again using material in Outline B, point out that the Quran indicates that Christians may be consulted. Also deal with the common Muslim objection that the Scriptures "that came before", which are the Old and New Testaments, have been changed and corrupted and are therefore unreliable. (See Chapter 12 and Appendix 2 for help with this.) Do not move too quickly from Quran to Bible here. It is vital for the Muslims you are addressing to follow the initial journey of ideas, something that is more likely to happen if phrased in terms familiar to them. For many, the objections to using the Bible are too strong just to skim over. You want to be able to get to a point where you can credibly say something like this:

> If Jesus is a prophet and something more than a prophet, it makes sense to find out about him in the place where there is information about him.

You may also wish to put out a challenge, such as the following:

> Until modern times, and still very widely, it has been true that most Muslims and Christians have been ignorant of each other's sacred books. This is a challenge to all of us. For now, we will look at Luke 24, chronologically the very last chapter of Luke's Gospel.

The Gospels and Jesus: Luke 24 and the double twist

Following the approach in Outline I, set the passage in context and make a connection between your hearers and the men who were grappling with the question of Jesus' identity. For example:

> These are questions relevant to Muslims today. You might think that the men in Luke 24 had had enough opportunity to find out who Jesus is – they have spent time with Jesus during his life and

ministry, have heard predictions of his death and resurrection, and know the importance of these predictions. But they are only human. Even his followers did not know what to make of him. There is no shame in holding Jesus in high honour and grappling with the question of exactly who he is.

Point out that Jesus gives an explanation of who he was, that forgiveness of sins is central to that explanation, and that the encounter with Jesus was ultimately satisfying. That is the double twist: forgiveness of sins becomes central, and joy replaces fear in the encounter.

Communicate how Jesus saw himself, and that it is important to make the effort to understand this. For this you may want to use some of the following:

- "Jesus' whole announcement of the kingdom of God indicates that he believed that kingdom to be present where he was, and operative through him personally. He believed that Israel's destiny was reaching its fulfilment in his life... Jesus, then, believed himself to be the focal point of the people of God."[74]

- "God's pardon is a free gift offered to everyone in spite of their sin and regardless of their merits. This gift can be offered without contradicting God's justice, because Jesus on the cross took upon himself the punishment for sin."[75]

Conclusions

At the start of your conclusion, you may wish to use a quotation such as the following:

"To state somewhat simply... that 'Jesus was merely a prophet' or that 'the Gospels have been corrupted' is to miss the point – rather like travelling at great expense and effort to Disneyland, taking a photo of the ticket booth, and returning home again, assuming that is all there is to see. Unless one can explain Jesus in terms of his historical background, understand what motivated him and drove him to follow through his vocation, and then explain how this gave birth to a new movement called 'Christianity', then it must be a case of back to the drawing board."[76]

Now summarize your talk so far.

Final thoughts: two challenges –

To Christians, remember the words of Jesus in Matthew 7:21–23. Why call him "Lord, Lord" and not do the things he says? To Muslims and others: what do you think of Christ?

The *Injil* and other New Testament material teach that if people do not respond to God's love, they will have to face his justice. Another part of the Bible says this:

In the past God overlooked such ignorance, but now he commands all people everywhere to repent. For he has set a day when he will judge the world with justice by the man he has appointed [this refers to Jesus]. He has given proof of this to all people by raising him from the dead.[77]

My purpose today has not been to prove Jesus' identity to you, but to leave you with the right questions. *'Isa* (the Arabic word for Jesus) is in heaven and knows the way to heaven. So consider the question: out of all the prophets, which one is best able to help us get to heaven?

Chapter 17

Tips for Bible study with a Muslim

The next six outlines assume that your Muslim friend is happy to use the Bible as a starting point for discussion. See Appendix 1 (Session 5) for abbreviated forms of some of the Bible studies.

Some of the outlines contain a lot of material. This is deliberate, as it allows you to pick and choose what is most helpful for the context in which you will use it. If you were to follow all the references in outlines D, E, F, and G in a one-to-one Bible study setting you would need two to four sessions, assuming you allowed enough time for questions and discussion (outlines H and I are shorter). So you may want to select just some of the references and some of the questions, to produce a one-session Bible study.[78]

Here are some tips on how to use the material to greatest effect, assuming you use it in a one-to-one Bible study format:

- Expect great things! *"The word of God is living and active. Sharper than any double-edged sword, it… judges the thoughts and attitudes of the heart."* (Hebrews 4:12)

- Make sure that you arrange to meet somewhere he or she will be happy to open the Bible and where you are not likely to keep being interrupted. For example, go to a quiet corner of a coffee shop or your living room after a meal.

- Prepare. Before leading the study, familiarize yourself with it, especially the context about Islam where given. This context will increase your awareness of where some Muslims are coming from in relation to the given topic. Spend half an hour in advance on your own looking up and reading every Bible passage referred to. This will allow you to choose which ones to use and how to divide the material in the outline into the number of sessions you desire.

- The core of Outlines D to G is where you see "Ask" and then a suggested question. Before getting to each question, you may need to read the suggested verses together and clarify and discuss whatever comes up. But it is the suggested questions that will move the conversation in a direction likely to be most helpful to Muslim seekers. I have presented outlines H and I in a more discursive way, allowing you to mould the material however you wish.

- Make sure you each have a Bible, preferably the same version and also a quite simple-to-read version, such as the NIV.

- Allow thirty to forty-five minutes for each instalment of the study. This time will go quickly, especially as those new to the Bible understandably require longer to find references there. Part of the time will be taken up dealing with introductory questions about the Bible as they arise.

- Although you should have a clear plan of what you will cover, don't be too rigid with your plan. Sometimes the most valuable discussions are the ones that veer off the topic. Sometimes you need to go with this flow.

- Pray! As appropriate, introduce the study with prayer and pray for insight and other needs as they arise. Perhaps most importantly, make sure you pray regularly outside the study for the important work you're doing.

Chapter 18

Starting from the Bible:
Outline D – Adam and Eve

Context about Islam for the leader of the study: Muslims believe that Adam was the first prophet. Adam is mentioned in six *suras* of the Quran. According to the Quran, Adam and Eve both ate the forbidden fruit and were banished from paradise (heaven) to earth. After they repented on earth, they were forgiven – Muslims do not subscribe to the concept of original sin. Also, some Muslims make a distinction between mistakes and sins. Prophets (according to their view) may make mistakes but are sinless – this includes Adam.

From Genesis 1:26 – 2:4, say that God created Adam. God was the source of life for Adam.

Read Genesis 2:15 – 3:8 together.

Ask: What are the results of sin? (Among the answers you are looking for is: "Sin produces death." Refer to Romans 3:23 at this point.)

Ask: In what ways is it clear that Adam and Eve felt shame for what they had done? (They tried to cover their nakedness and they tried to hide from God.)

Read Genesis 3:9–24 together.

Ask: What happened to Adam and Eve that day? (They didn't die physically, but they were separated from God.)

Ask: How effective were Adam and Eve's attempts to cover their shame? (Useless.)

Read Mark 10:45 and John 19:16–30 together. Discuss the significance of Jesus' death on the cross in the light of the facts raised earlier. Recall from Genesis that death means separation from God, who is our source of life. Make the link with shame and honour: Jesus' death sets us free from shame.

Read Romans 5:14–15 and 6:23 together.

Ask: Did Jesus sin? Did God need to penalize Jesus as he did Adam and Eve? Make the point that in Romans 5–6 another free gift – a greater one, eternal life – is on offer from God.

Chapter 19

Starting from the Bible: Outline E – Abraham

Context about Islam for the leader of the study: Abraham is known as the friend of God in Islam. His name appears sixty-nine times in the Quran. Following in the footsteps of Abraham is very important to Muslims. Muslims believe that the son Abraham offered up for sacrifice was Ishmael, not Isaac. In what follows, I recommend not making much of this difference in views between Muslims and Christians. More important is to make the point that a sacrifice was needed and that God provided it.

Read Genesis 12:1–3 together. By way of context, say that this passage comes after one which makes it clear that the world was full of false ideas and confusion.

Ask: What was God's plan to deal with this situation? (Raising up a people through whom God would reveal his blessing.)

Read Genesis 15:1–6 and 17:1–8 together. Explain that Abram had become too old to have a child. (The reason for Abram/Abraham's name change is in 17:5 – it was to reaffirm the covenant God made.)

Ask: What did God promise Abram? What was Abram's response, and on what basis did God count him righteous? (The basis was Abram's belief.)

Read Genesis 22:1–14 together. (If appropriate, say that this was also the place where, according to Christian tradition, the crucifixion took place.)

Ask: What do you think of Abraham's obedience? Who provided the sacrifice in the end?

Now **read** Romans 4:1–5 and John 3:16 together.

Ask: According to this, on what basis can someone get right with God? Depending on how the discussion proceeds, look at passages on Jesus' death and resurrection, such as Mark 15:22 – 16:8, and bring a personal challenge to your friend, perhaps based on John 1:12. Other relevant Bible passages on Abraham include James 2:23 (Abraham as the friend of God) and Galatians 3:6–9 (Abraham and the importance of faith).

Chapter 20
_____
Starting from the Bible:
Outline F – Moses

Context about Islam for the leader of the study: The name of Moses is the most frequently occurring of all the Islamic prophets in the Quran. The Quran teaches that Allah spoke directly to Moses (something not said of Muhammad). Muslims think that Moses' life and work as a messenger, lawgiver, and leader most closely foreshadows that of Muhammad.

Read Exodus 12:1–6 and 21–27 together. Depending on the background knowledge of your friend, you may need to give some background, for example covering slavery in Egypt, God's raising up of Moses, the plagues, and the deliverance of God's people. Then say that for his people Israel, God put in place a sacrifice system (verses 6 and 21).

Ask: What kind of sacrifice was it? (Verse 5 – without defect.)

Ask: What was necessary for God's people to perform the sacrifice? (Various answers can be given, including obedience and the slaughter of the animal.)

Ask: What kind of animal needed to be slaughtered? (Verse 21 – a lamb.)

Summarize by saying that in order to be right with God, his people at that time had to bring such offerings. This system was in operation for the 1,500 years leading up to and including the time of Jesus. God's people were frequently reminded of a lamb that had died in their place.

Now **read** John 1:29.

Ask: What did John the Baptist call Jesus? (The Lamb of God, who takes away the sin of the world.)

Read 1 Peter 1:17–20.

Ask: What similarities are there between this description and the story from Exodus? (A lamb, without blemish, for redemption.)

As before, depending on where the discussion has reached, make the connection between our sins, the need for sacrifice, and Jesus' provision of that sacrifice. Perhaps use Romans 3:21–6 and/ or one of the cross-related passages recommended in outlines D and E.[79]

Chapter 21

Starting from the Bible: Outline G – the Samaritans

This approach is particularly effective for use with Muslim friends who have had negative experiences with Christians, for example where they have been personally offended by their approach.[80] Rather than taking a sin–penalty–cross approach, as the three previous character-based outlines do, this outline creates the conditions for further fruitful discussion by affirming Jesus' desire to include people.

Below are several mini Bible studies. At the start of each one, you may need to give some background as to why the Samaritans are relevant to this situation. That background is: Jesus and many of his early followers were Jews. The Samaritans were monotheists with different views to the Jews, and intense communal hostility existed between them and the Jews. In some ways, perhaps Jewish–Samaritan conflict in the New Testament is a parallel for some aspects of Christian–Muslim conflict today?

Read Luke 9:51–56 together.

Ask: How does Jesus respond to the disciples who are seeking aggressive judgment? (Jesus rebukes them.)

Ask: How does Jesus respond to Samaritan hostility? (Graciously.) Discuss the contrast of Jesus' treatment of the Samaritans with that of the disciples and what it tells you of Jesus' love. (He loves those who don't yet know him. His love is not a weak thing.)

Read Luke 17:11–19 together.

Say: Jesus physically heals the Samaritan and commends the Samaritan's gratitude.

Ask: What impact do you think that had on hearers? Discuss what this tells you about who Jesus wants to follow him.

Read John 4:1–42 together.

Say: On meeting the woman at the well, Jesus crosses the barriers of gender and religion, to the surprise of the woman and of Jesus' disciples.

Ask: Where does Jesus challenge her and what about?

Say: Jesus is inclusive here in many ways, but not at the expense of sharing truth in a relevant manner. So, he also challenges the Samaritan woman over issues of truth.

Ask: What might Jesus challenge me and you about today?

In conjunction with the above, you may wish to point to other Samaritan-relevant passages, such as:

Luke 10:29–37, where Jesus uses the despised Samaritan as the model for loving others, no doubt to the irritation of at least some of his listeners.

Acts 1:8 and 9:31, where Jesus includes the despised Samaria in the places where the disciples will be his witnesses, and where Samaria is noted as one of the places where the church was growing.

Chapter 22

Starting from the Bible:
Outline H – The parable of the tenants

The vast majority of Muslims in the West come from cultures where honour and shame are very important. This is different from much of Western culture, where concepts of guilt and freedom tend to dominate thinking much more. Engaging with the honour–shame paradigm is therefore important. This outline illustrates one aspect of how you might do this.

Picture the scene: Lebanon, 2011. A successful vineyard owner has to make a long visit to California for family reasons, so he temporarily rents his network of vineyards out to some local farmers, on the understanding that they will share the proceeds of the harvest. But come harvest time, the farmers sell the grapes via the local cooperative and pocket all the cash. When the vineyard owner sends an agent to collect his money, one of the farmers shoots the agent. The vineyard owner sends another agent, and then another, because he cannot afford to lose his livelihood. But the farmers continue their killing spree, and even dump the bodies in open sewers by the streets for all to see. The owner has a son, and decides to raise the stakes in the most dramatic way possible: by sending him to collect his share of the harvest. The owner sweated blood over this decision, but felt he had no other choice.

Now, put yourself in the shoes of the son. How would you feel as you were about to be sent on this mission? Afraid of what the tenants might do to you? Tempted to reason with your father, to see whether there could be another way? Even if the honour of your family were very important to you, would you really want to go through with such a request? I'm not sure I would.

A story like the one above is told in the New Testament in Matthew 21:33–44, and the son in that story did honour his father by going on the mission. This son stands for Jesus. The Gospels of Matthew, Mark, Luke, and John are full of stories and teaching relating to how Jesus honoured his Father. The rest of the New Testament also affirms that Jesus honoured his Father greatly.

Overall, the Bible teaches that Jesus honoured his Father much more than just by going on a business errand, even an important business errand. Jesus was so morally unblemished that even when his enemies in the Sanhedrin, as well as the chief priests, searched high and low for evidence to convict him, they couldn't find any.[81] To maintain his Father's honour, Jesus even took on himself the shame of others. That is, his obedience stretched even as far as being falsely accused and wrongly punished, giving his life that others might receive honour. Why should we not honour Jesus for this? After all, rewarding his obedience, the Father raised Jesus up and gave him the highest honour.

To take this a step further you might go on to talk about the shame of our own sin and our shameful treatment of Jesus, if we do not honour him for who he is. (Notice how the story ends in Matthew 21:43–44.) You might contrast our shame with Jesus' honour, adding that we were all enemies of God, but that Jesus took our hatred and sin on himself and responded by forgiving us and honouring us instead. Why should we not honour Jesus for his honourable death even despite our shameful behaviour towards him?

Chapter 23

Starting from the Bible:
Outline I – Resurrection appearances

This outline is an example of how to explain the relevance of Jesus as one fulfilling what previous prophets foretold. It is therefore complementary to the earlier outlines relating to Adam and Eve, Abraham, and Moses.

The New Testament contains an intriguing story of two men who, though they held Jesus in high honour and thought he was a prophet, don't know quite what to make of him. As Luke introduces this story in his Gospel, the two men have just been discussing Jesus' crucifixion and resurrection (e.g. Luke 23:44–46 and 24:1–11). Jesus comes along and asks them about the things that have happened. The story goes on:

"What things?" he asked. "About Jesus of Nazareth," they replied. "He was a prophet, powerful in word and deed before God and all the people. The chief priests and our rulers handed him over to be sentenced to death, and they crucified him; but we had hoped that he was the one who was going to redeem Israel. And what is more, it is the third day since all this took place. In addition, some of our women amazed us. They went to the tomb early this morning but didn't find his body. They came and told us that they had seen a vision of angels, who said he was alive. Then some of our companions went to the tomb and found it just as the women had said, but him they did not see" (Luke 24:19–24).

We are then told that *"beginning with Moses and all the Prophets, he explained to them what was said in all the Scriptures concerning himself"* (Luke 24:27). We are not given the details of Jesus' explanations of how the Scriptures point to him. But the drama of the story in Luke 24 and the sweeping nature of the topics Jesus covers (for example, prophethood and forgiveness of sins) tell us that something important is going on. To clarify what this is, let's reflect on a vital incident that illuminates Luke's (and other Gospel writers') treatment of prophethood and forgiveness of sins.

Picture another scene: Jesus is at a meal with his disciples before his arrest, trial, and crucifixion. He and his disciples have just broken bread. Jesus offers a cup of wine and, in a statement full of symbolism, says, *"This is my blood of the covenant, which is poured out for many for the forgiveness of sins."*[82] The words *"for many"* provide a link to Isaiah 53:11, where God's servant is to suffer in place of all those to whom the benefits of his death would apply. That is, the greatest hopes of the Old Testament find fulfilment in Jesus in the New Testament.[83] And Jesus said and did some things that drew attention to himself as a focus of history.

In other words, the New Testament does not just present previous prophetic promises as coming true in and through Jesus' own life and ministry, but also makes it clear that Jesus understood this to be the case. Jesus is not just saying, "I am a messenger," but is in some way pointing to himself, not others. To adapt N. T. Wright's phrase (used in Outline C), Jesus believed that the destiny of the people of God was reaching its fulfilment in his own life. That is the context in which we read in Luke 24:49, *"I am going to send you what my Father has promised."*

These understandings reflect the early Christian conviction that the Scriptures witness pervasively to Jesus and to the way in which his life unfolded. Six hundred years before Muhammad, Jesus saw himself as the turning point in the narrative of history, somebody who was good news for all.

In Luke 24, upon understanding in a new way who Jesus was, the hearts of these (early) followers of Jesus burned within them. His closest followers in time and place also came to understand these things when they heard Jesus explain them. In the same way, it is possible today for Muslims and others to know that forgiveness of sins is one of God's greatest blessings – an undeserved, wonderful gift that, according to Jesus, comes only through him.

The Jesus to whom the Gospels refer is one who can do the impossible. In the story from Luke 24, joy ultimately replaced fear for Jesus' followers. Sometimes, when people initially appreciate who Jesus is, they are startled, perhaps afraid and even ashamed. For those who repent and trust him for forgiveness of sins through his work on the cross, Jesus can remove fear, shame, and lack of understanding. Maybe this seems impossible to you, but Jesus can do it.

Chapter 24

Starting from festivals:
Outline J – Why Christmas?

This outline is based on a talk I delivered in December 2007 in the UK to a mixed audience including several local Muslims who had heard about the event on the radio. The event, organized by a local church, took place in a community centre. There were mince pies, non-alcoholic drinks, live music, and a short talk explaining what Christians mean by Christmas. The talk lasted about fifteen minutes and was designed to be accessible to people of many different backgrounds, not just Muslims. Before the talk, there was a performance song, "Mary's boy child", and Matthew 1:18–25 was read aloud.

There are many ways you could run an event similar to this. You could ask guests of different nationalities to provide food from their nations. You could put on carols, poetry, or other entertainment instead of (or as well as) a performance song. Someone could tell a story of what God means to them.

The reason why I have provided notes rather than a verbatim text for the talk is that everybody's style is different and your talk will be most effective if you make it your own.

Introduction

There are various ways to introduce this talk. Tell funny stories about your own Christmas experiences. Or, as I did, use a box full of props. Be creative with what you use. I used a Santa hat, a carrier bag, a wrapped present, a vegetarian Christmas pudding and a calendar with the dates 25 and 26 December circled.

What does Christmas mean to you? Maybe Santa [show hat]. In Derry in Ireland last December, there were 13,000 Santas trying to break the world record for the number of Santas in a fun run. Or does it mean shopping [show carrier bag]? Or for children, or all those young at heart – presents [show wrapped present]. Or food [show Christmas pudding] – did you know that sales of indigestion tablets go through the roof at Christmas? Those of you who work [show calendar] – either breathe a huge sigh of relief at having two extra days off or will be back-breakingly busy if you are in retail or the catering trade.

The thing about Christmas is that it has come to mean all of these things. I love mince pies and other Christmas foods. I enjoy buying presents for my friends and family.

But when it comes down to it, what do Christians mean by Christmas? Although we're all aware of these other meanings [wave box], as Ralph W. Sockman said "The hinge of history is found on the door of a Bethlehem stable." Christmas, **Christ**mas, Christ, "This is how the birth of Jesus Christ came about" (verse 18). Christmas is traditionally a time to reflect on the significance of the birth of Jesus Christ.

I want to highlight two reasons why Jesus' birth is significant for all. First, quite obviously:

Jesus' birth gave rise to his life – this is wonderful for us all as a community.

Quote the song: "Mary's boy child Jesus Christ was born on Christmas Day."

The focus is not on Mary, but on her boy, Jesus Christ, this child who was born and lived a wonderful life.

Ask those who wouldn't call themselves Christians to think about the following:

- The Hindu Swami Vivekananda praised Jesus as the epitome of perfection.
- The Quran calls him righteous, a healer, and one to be obeyed.
- The overwhelming majority of Western scholars not only agree that Jesus was born but also credit his extraordinary teachings to him.

  He never had a house, never held office, never led an army, but the birth and life of Jesus has influenced and continues to inspire billions worldwide today. Why?

- In a world full of pride, Jesus served, going the extra mile, washing his followers' feet.
- In a world full of sickness, Jesus healed the sick.
- In a world crying out for peace and full of spiritual desire, Jesus said, "Blessed are the peacemakers, for they will be called sons of God."

  Take peace, for example. Here in the Cowley Road area, we have increasing numbers of community police officers and are shortly to get surveillance cameras, reflecting increased crime. Nationally and internationally, these are tense times among many communities.

  How we need a man of peace to follow! We can celebrate together, whatever background we're from, that Jesus was a man of peace. This is something we can reflect on together, and share in this Christmas: the wonderful news that Jesus Christ was born, and lived, giving so much to humanity.

[Recap talk so far]

Jesus' birth tells us that he came to save us from our sins – this is important for us all personally.

[Refer back to song] "And man will live for evermore, because of Christmas Day."

Tell some funny and/or poignant stories that will illustrate the power and reality of sin. For example, I retold part of the story of former gangster Nicky Cruz (related in the book *Run Baby Run*), ending with the part where, dramatically, he realized that Jesus really loved him. Here is how I transitioned from the end of the story to the rest of the talk.

> "You are to give him the name Jesus, because he will save his people from their sins" (Matthew 1:21). Because he asked Jesus for forgiveness, Nicky Cruz received it and was saved from his sins. As Christians reflect on the meaning of Christmas, the story of the birth of Jesus not only reminds us of his wonderful life, but also of the fact that he came to save us from our sins through his death on the cross.
>
> Nicky Cruz never looked back from handing in his gun and deciding to follow Jesus. Jesus spoke of giving life in all its fullness. As it says in his book, "Nicky Cruz traded in the quick release of adrenaline in the gang culture for happiness evermore."[84]
>
> The wrong things we do are the things that separate us from God. These are the things that need to be forgiven for us to relate properly to God. Sin is the barrier, and Jesus was announced as the one who would remove that barrier.
>
> In fact, the name Jesus is derived from the word meaning "The Lord saves."
>
> Being saved from our sins is good news for our community too.

Depending on timings and your preferred approach, consider adding a section that affirms that the whole Bible points in the direction of the above conclusions. For example, emphasize that the prophets foretold the importance of Jesus' birth for saving people from their sins, that this fact was reinforced during his life, and that this same fact applies to us today.

Conclusion

This is what Christians mean by Christmas. A time of joy. A time of remembering, especially that the birth of Jesus speaks of peace and reconciliation.

His life of peace and purity – a wonderful blessing for our community.

His ultimate death and the fact that he came to save us from our sins – important news personally for each of us.

One final thought before we eat together: Christmas is one of the greatest festivals of the year. Many years ago, at another great festival, Jesus stood up and said, "If anyone is thirsty, let him come to me and drink. Whoever believes in me, as the Scripture has said, streams of living water will flow from within him." It's as if Jesus were saying, "Some things are not essential (presents, Christmas pudding). One thing that is essential to the body is water. In the same way, if you are thirsty of soul, it is essential that you come to me, Jesus, and drink."

Part 4

Hot potatoes: Some questions arising for Christians on aspects of Islam

There are hundreds of questions that Christians ask about reaching Muslims. Many of these questions are "hot potato questions" – particularly tough to handle.

In an introductory book such as this it is very important to prioritize. So this section contains the three hot potato questions that in my experience Christians most commonly ask when thinking about connecting with Muslims.

For books and websites dealing with other questions, please see Appendix 2.

Chapter 25

Should Christians call God "Allah"?

The question "Should Christians call God 'Allah'?" arises because of the strong association of the word "Allah" with the Muslim God, in the minds of many English-speakers. This is an understandable association, since most English-speakers will only ever have heard the word used in the context of Islam.

Allāh ("Allah") is the Arabic word for God. Millions of Arabic-speaking Christians worldwide use the word, along with other words such as *rabb* (Arabic for Lord), to refer to God. In this linguistic sense, it is no different from a French-speaking Christian using the word *Dieu* or a German *Gott*. In his address to the Athenians at the Areopagus, the apostle Paul used the Greek word *theos* to refer both to the Athenians' unknown god and to his own God. *Theos* was and is a word for God used by Greek-speaking Christians when worshipping him.[85] On grounds such as these, I do not have a problem with the use, by Christians in a worship context, of the word "Allah". And, if I am talking with a Muslim and he or she refers to Allah, I would not generally be aiming to get him or her to stop using the word.

We must also be clear on the related theological issues. The Christian's understanding of the character of God is quite different from that of a Muslim. Even though there are things in common, such as the facts that he is powerful or pre-existent, we should not allow important distinctives to be swept under the carpet simply because of the fact that Muslims as well as some Christians use the word "Allah".[86]

The two paragraphs above have highlighted differences between the linguistic and theological aspects of the question "Should Christians call God 'Allah'?" There is another closely related question that also illustrates these differences: "Do Christians and Muslims worship the same God?" (See box.)

Do Christians and Muslims worship the same God?

Colin Chapman helpfully says that this is a kind of trick question. On the one hand, of course there are things in common between Christian and Muslim understandings of God. So perhaps we could answer yes, it is the same God being worshipped. But on the other hand, there are real differences. So perhaps we could answer no, it is not the same God being worshipped. Any answer to this tricky question deserves care.

Christians from a Muslim background sometimes say that when they were Muslims, they had some real knowledge of God that Jesus then brought into focus in a new way when they became Christians. As Colin Chapman points out, "Bilquis Sheikh in *I Dared to Call Him Father* points to continuity rather than discontinuity."[87] This is important to affirm.

However, few people claim that the Christian God and the Muslim God are exactly the same. It may be that one sheds light on the other, but what we must avoid is a logically absurd situation where incompatible claims are held as compatible. Let me explain by taking as an example God's method of salvation, specifically how one gets to heaven or paradise. For Christians, this happens through repentance and faith in Jesus. For Muslims, the main way this happens is when on the day of judgment God judges your good deeds to have outweighed your bad deeds. These are different and, I would suggest, mutually exclusive methods of salvation.

So let's be open about the fact that the Christian and Muslim deities, as defined within each faith, have differences. These differences are fundamental and mutually exclusive, not superficial and somehow logically reconcilable. I have personally found that frank recognition of this fact leads to greater openness in communication on both sides about what each person admires and wants to challenge about the other's life and faith. While as Christians we can affirm the monotheism of Muslims, we cannot affirm their view of God in totality. Finally, while not wanting to duck the above discussion, I would also urge reframing the question along lines such as, "What is similar and what is different about Christian and Muslim understandings of Jesus?"

Underlying all the above material is the critical issue of contextualization. Imagine you are talking with a British English-speaking Christian teenager with no Muslim background. If that teenager inexplicably started referring to God as "Allah", of course that would be odd and you should address the issue. But if an Arabic-speaking Christian uses the word "Allah" it is important not to be surprised and not to try to change it. Now consider another situation entirely, such as where the imposition of Islam in another country led to the word "Allah" being strongly associated with the Muslim God. In such cases (e.g. Turkey) many Christians refrain from using the word "Allah", preferring *Tanrı* (Turkish for "God"). Also many would use *rabb* (Lord) or other alternatives. These usages too are OK. If you meet such Christians, do not try to persuade them to use the word "Allah", thinking that the above linguistic points about *theos* somehow outweigh their decisions.[88]

Also, in the West many Muslims are from non-English- and non-Arabic-speaking backgrounds (for example Urdu speakers in the UK). For the Urdu speaker who does not know Arabic, "Allah" represents an Islamic view of God and nothing else. Christians from such backgrounds may also want to steer well clear of using the word "Allah". Finally, a helpful tip for when you are in conversation with Muslims (or Christians from a Muslim background) may be to use a phrase similar to the one that David Pawson has often recommended in such situations: "The God and Father of our Lord Jesus."

In summary, while there is no compelling theological reason

why Arabic-speaking Christians cannot in principle use the word "Allah" of God, the context may dictate avoiding use of the term for the Christian God, especially for some non-Arabic-speaking Christians.

Chapter 26

When should baptism happen?

If a Muslim becomes a Christian and is then persecuted, this persecution is often most intense around the time of baptism (or the prior discussion of it among the former Muslim's family or friends).[89] In one sense this is understandable, as baptism is a highly visible physical symbol[90] that involves giving up the old (a dying to the former self) and identifying with the new (a rising with Christ). So decisions about baptism (not just whether to do it, but the timing, location and other practical issues) can be incredibly difficult. Stated more precisely, the question here is: When should a former Muslim who has become a Christian be baptized?

Let me outline some principles based on biblical teaching in relation to this matter. First, Jesus spoke of the great cost of following him.[91] Yes, the reward is greater, but the size of the cost should not surprise us. We are sometimes insulated from this reality or do not notice it in the West. Second, there is no indication in the New Testament that believers are permitted to decline ever to be baptized on the grounds of family or other difficulties it may cause. We must be very sensitive here. Technically Muslims who become Christians are committing apostasy and blasphemy. From the perspective of Muslims, this is serious. Therefore, the need for care (and sometimes protection) for Christians from Muslim backgrounds is acute. Especially post-baptism, we must be ready as churches to do whatever it takes to support former Muslims. Third, when someone becomes a Christian, the baptism should usually happen relatively quickly.[92] Ordinarily, this should apply to a former Muslim.

However, it is not possible to legislate for every eventuality, even given the above principles. To some extent, how one should proceed does depend on the individual, for example in respect of the strength of their family connections. To help answer the above question practically, it is important to consider what is often a key underlying question: When can I know that a Muslim has become a Christian? Recognizing that only God truly knows the answer to this, below is some general guidance that in my view is consistent with the above biblical explanations about following Jesus. (Note: the criteria below do not require that much time has elapsed since profession of faith.)

Some pointers that help us discern when a Muslim has become a Christian and may be ready for baptism:[93]

- They can say "Jesus is Lord" and understand what that means.

- They can renounce the tenets of Islam in the sense that Muhammad is God's prophet, with all that that means.

- A life of discipleship has started, which is evidenced in change such as an understanding of grace and the first loyalty being to Christ, not the family (the family to be honoured without it ruling).

Even the above guidelines are complex. For example, what does it mean in practice to renounce Muhammad as prophet in your life? What should one depart from or affirm in particular cases? There are no easy answers here.

One radical answer sometimes given is for Christians from Muslim backgrounds to continue operating as Muslims (even though they now follow Jesus) in their own communities, including worshipping at their mosque. This is usually justified with reference to claimed long-term benefits of reaching family and friends in Muslim communities. (Sometimes this is called "the insider movement".) This model may be problematic in that sometimes it can downplay the radical change involved at conversion. However, it often involves a powerful move of God, and it is vital we recognize the real challenges that have given rise to its usually well intentioned approaches.[94]

For example, coming out of Islam can be complex, and the cost of following Jesus openly can be very high. Also, Muslim background believers should not jettison every aspect of their previous culture and upbringing. (God forbid that Muslim background believers should all start dressing like non-Muslims!) Often new disciples just need time to work through issues such as baptism or their new identity in Christ. That is fine as an interim step, and in some cases this may mean a delay in a baptism happening. Overall we should be uncomfortable with a long-term, stable situation in which a Christian (who is a former Muslim) continues to operate essentially as a practising Muslim.

Finally, in making decisions about baptisms beware several things. First, some asylum seekers see baptism as a passport to citizenship. Some churches have found it helpful to delay baptism deliberately for that group, to test the authenticity of the profession of faith. Once fruit is seen, baptism follows. Second, baptism is not necessarily an evangelistic opportunity, and a private baptism may be appropriate in some cases. There is no evidence of a crowd around the Ethiopian eunuch in Acts 8. Third, let us not require of Muslim background believers anything that is out of proportion with what we require of believers from other backgrounds. The worst manifestation of this would be a two-tier baptism system where the former face dozens of extra hurdles that the latter don't. Rather, ensure that baptism is a cherished and seriously considered step for who become Christians.

Chapter 27

Is it OK for Christians to eat halal meat?

From around the eighth century AD onwards, the dominant meaning of the Arabic legal term *halāl* came to be "lawful".[95] Today, Muslims understand halal meat as that which is lawful for them to eat, because of factors such as prayer said around the time of killing, the qualifications of the butcher, and the way in which the animal is killed. That is, in the act of killing the animal, it has been offered to the Muslim God.

One traditional Christian response to whether Christians can eat such meat is "No". This response is often justified by citing Acts 15, a chapter which starts with a description of a dispute about whether new Gentile believers in Antioch, Syria, and Cilicia should be circumcised. Involved in the discussions were Paul and Barnabas, the party of the Pharisees, and apostles and elders in Jerusalem. The occasion is sometimes known as the Council of Jerusalem. After deliberating, the apostles and elders decided (among other things) to send a letter to the Gentile believers which included the words: "You are to abstain from food sacrificed to idols" (Acts 15:29; see also Acts 21:25).

In contrast to this, my response to the above question is, "Yes it is OK for Christians to eat halal meat, as long as by so doing they are not causing another to stumble spiritually." My view is based not so much on questioning the validity of equating "idol" with "Muslim God",[96] but rather on what I see as a more rounded consideration of the biblical material on idolatry, in which believers seem to have great freedom in Christ (see detailed explanation in the box below).

ADVANCED

THE RELATION OF BIBLICAL MATERIAL ON IDOLATRY TO THE QUESTION OF HALAL MEAT

The biblical material against idolatry takes many forms and occurs in many contexts. In his book The Mission of God: Unlocking the Bible's Grand Narrative, *in a section entitled "Confronting idolatry",[97] Christopher Wright highlights four different approaches which are apparent in the writings of the apostle Paul, among other places. The four approaches are: forthrightness when engaged in dense theological argument,[98] a context-dependent approach when speaking evangelistically,[99] exposing and denouncing idolatry, in particular when warning the people of God prophetically,[100] and pastoral guidance. Since the question for this chapter, as well as Acts 15, relates mostly to this fourth category of pastoral guidance, let us now consider it in more detail.*

Acts 15 does not exhaust the biblical material on pastoral guidance in the context of idolatry. 1 Corinthians 8–10 is also a central passage to consider here. The apostle Paul seems to leave us in no doubt: "So then, about eating food sacrificed to idols: We know that an idol is nothing at all in the world" (1 Corinthians 8:4) and, "Eat anything sold in the meat market without raising questions of conscience, for, 'The earth is the Lord's, and everything in it'" (1 Corinthians 10:25–26). Also, note the important words, "Be careful, however, that the exercise of your freedom does not become a stumbling block to the weak" (1 Corinthians 8:9; see also verse 13). Taking this together, the radical freedom that believers have in Christ goes hand in hand with the law of love that compels them not to do things detrimental to others. In addition, based on these passages from 1 Corinthians, Christopher Wright makes what I believe is a helpful and important distinction between buying meat from the ordinary meat market (no problem for Christians to do, even if it has been previously offered to other gods) and participating in sacrifices to other gods in the precincts of the temples of the gods ("Flee from idolatry," as Paul puts it).

Finally, we must not mistake the effect the Acts 15 letter was expected to have on the young Gentile church. On hearing the law emphasis of those representing the Pharisees in Acts 15:5 ("The Gentiles must be circumcised and required to obey the law of Moses"), Peter disagreed by pointing to the centrality for salvation of faith and the grace of the Lord Jesus Christ, and to the fact that the Gentiles have been included in this. James adds, "We should not make it difficult for the Gentiles who are turning to God" (Acts 15:19). Both Peter and James position their arguments within the history of God's saving actions among his people (prophecy from Amos 9 and narrative from Acts 10). The impact on the Gentiles of a letter with such a short list of conditions would have been (expected to be) huge. This is indicated by the nature of the discussions the apostles had before deciding to send the letter. Previously, many in the God-fearing world had believed circumcision and other ritual requirements were necessary to establish and maintain a relationship with God. Now, as Peter and James had recently discovered, the offer of grace through faith, which means such laws are no longer necessary for salvation, extended also to Gentiles.

If one were somehow to ban Christians from eating halal meat, the implications would be massive. The following question of course does not decide the issue, but consider this: Would you be comfortable saying that anyone converting from Islam can never eat with their family (or even spouse) again? Surely this is the very kind of unnecessary obstacle which Acts 15 sets out to avoid. We would also be presenting Christianity as a religion steeped in legalism and rule-keeping, surely the thing that Jesus refuses to do in Mark 7:19.[101] Also, you may yourself be inadvertently eating halal meat, as seventy branches of the KFC fast food chain in the UK use it, as do several

McDonald's restaurants in the USA, in Australia, and elsewhere across the world.[102]

Sometimes the issue of halal meat becomes an aspect of power politics. It is a good thing to be sensitive in providing food for Muslim guests that they are comfortable eating, including halal food. However, it is a different matter if Muslims you are hosting insist on halal-only cuisine even for non-Muslims that are there. (This has occasionally happened.) Although you may want to agree to this second request for a time – I think that would be wise in some circumstances – you should challenge it at some point, partly to foster a greater spirit of honour on all sides.

Overall, for a Christian it is fine to eat halal meat, as long as your action does not cause another to stumble. In this area, it is important that we do not allow our faith to be eroded since, as Christopher Wright puts it, there is a "paradox that although gods and idols are *something* in the world, they are *nothing* in comparison to the living God".[103]

Conclusion

Congratulations! You have made it to the end of the main part of this book. Your journey of understanding maps, seeking open hearts, helping people see afresh, and dealing with hot potatoes is complete – or is it?

Of course not. Many Muslims are passionate about faith and truth. So go and make friends with them. Welcome, accept, and level with them. Every encounter will be different, because every Muslim is different. Remember that God goes ahead of you. Never underestimate what God has done and is doing in the lives of your Muslim friends. Never underestimate what God has done and is doing in your life, to make you ready for your next encounter. And enjoy putting this book into practice.

Glossary of terms

The Quran has 114 sections (each section is called a *sura*) and each *sura* is made up of verses (the verse is called an *aya*). A reference such as Q9:29 refers to the twenty-ninth *aya* in the ninth *sura* of the Quran.

This glossary gives both the form used in this book (in bold) and the form as transliterated from the Arabic (see below for an explanation of this).

Allah – *allāh* – The Arabic word for "God" (see *rabb*).

Aya – *āya* – Literally, "sign". Nearly always means a verse of the Quran.

Bid'a – *bid'a* – (plural *bida'*) Innovation. *Bid'a* is almost always considered bad by Muslims, who strive to be traditional in the sense of following what Muhammad (and sometimes his early companions) said and did.

Burqa – *burqa* – A type of head-covering. See Chapter 4.

Eid – *'īd* – A festival. The two most commonly known are Eid al-Fitr (which marks the end of Ramadan) and Eid al-Adha (sometimes called the festival of sacrifice, which takes place in the Islamic month of Dhu al-Hijja).

Hadith – *hadīth* – Reports (individual or collected) of what Muhammad said and did.

Hajj – *hajj* – Pilgrimage to Mecca. One of the five pillars of Islam, which Muslims are expected to keep.

Halal – *halāl* – "Permissible" or "lawful", a term used in Islamic jurisprudence and applicable not just to meat but also to almost every other aspect of life and conduct.

Hijab – *hijāb* – a type of head-covering. See Chapter 4.

Injil – *injīl* – Arabic word for the Gospels. The word is used in the Quran.

Islam – *islām* – Literally, "submission" or "surrender", not "peace" as is sometimes claimed (see *salam*).

Jihad – *jihād* – Literally, "struggle". Muslims tend to agree that the word refers to a spiritual struggle of some kind. Some Muslims emphasize the interior, devotional aspects of *jihād*. Others emphasize the physical and militaristic aspects, which are abundantly present in the Islamic writings of the centuries following Muhammad's death.

Mecca – *makka* – The holiest city, according to Islam. Muslims are expected to face in its direction when praying.

Medina – *madīna* – The second holiest city, according to Islam. According to the traditional Muslim narrative, Muhammad moved to Medina after having left Mecca.

Muhammad – *muḥammad* – Literally, "one who is praised". A common name among Muslims, it was also the name of the founder of Islam.

Muslim – *muslim* – Literally, "one who submits".

Niqab – *niqāb* – a type of head-covering. See Chapter 4.

Quran – *qur'ān* – Literally, "recitation". The holy book that Muslims revere most.

Rabb – *rabb* – The Arabic word for "Lord" (see *Allah*).

Ramadan – *ramaḍān* – The ninth month of the Islamic lunar calendar, in which *sawm* takes place in daylight hours. Many Muslims believe that this fast covers food, water, and sexual intercourse.

Salam – *salām* – Literally, "peace". The word comes from the same root as the Arabic word *islām*. The greeting "*salām alaykum*" means "Peace be upon you" and is a common greeting among Arabic speakers, as well as some non-Arabic-speaking Muslims. A common response is the reciprocal "*wa alaykum salām*" – "And upon you be peace."

Salat – *ṣalāt* – Prayer. One of the five pillars of Islam, which Muslims are expected to keep.

Sawm – *ṣawm* – Fasting. One of the five pillars of Islam, which Muslims are expected to keep, for example during Ramadan.

Shahada – *shahāda* – The Muslim creed. One of the five pillars of

Islam, which Muslims are expected to say. Saying it with a sincere heart for the first time makes someone a Muslim.

Shi'i – *shī'ī* – Often referred to as Shi'i, Shi'ite or Shi'a Muslims, this group forms approximately 10 per cent of the global Muslim population. They believe that members of Muhammad's family and descendants are the rightful spiritual and political rulers of Islam, starting with Ali, Muhammad's cousin and son-in-law. They have split into various sects, including Zaydis, Ismailis, and Imamis.

Sira – *sīra* – Literally, "way". Came to mean "biography", among other things. Most commonly relates to biographies of the prophet Muhammad. The best known version is *Sīrat rasūl allāh,* by Ibn Isḥāq (d. AD 761 or 767), available only via a work by Ibn Hishām (d. AD 833), whose version of Ibn Isḥāq's work was famously said to have been abbreviated, annotated, and sometimes altered.

Sufi – *ṣūfī* – Sufi Muslims generally follow a more mystical and/or ascetic form of faith. Many Sufis advocate using tombs of saints as places of worship, whereas many other Muslims reject such practices. Some Sunnis and Shi'is also consider themselves Sufis, whereas some do not.

Sunna – *sunna* – Literally, "usual practice" or "habit". In Muslim discourse, the term generally refers to what Muhammad said and did.

Sunni – *sunnī* – Often referred to as Sunni or Sunnite Muslims, this group forms approximately 85 per cent of the global Muslim population. They consider Ali to have been the fourth rightful leader of the Muslim community after Muhammad.

Sura – *sūra* – Refers to a section or chapter of the Quran.

Tawrat – *tawrāt* – Arabic word relating to the Pentateuch. Muslims often use this word to refer to the Old Testament or Jewish beliefs more generally. The word is used in the Quran.

Umma – *umma* – Literally "community" or "nation", often used in the context of Islam to refer to the global community of believers.

Zabur – *zabūr* – Arabic word for the Psalms. The word is used in the Quran.

Zakat – *zakāt* – Giving to the poor. One of the five pillars of Islam, which Muslims are expected to keep.

In case you are wondering about the strange dots underneath, and horizontal lines above, some letters, here is the short explanation (not for the technically faint-hearted!). Each character, be it "ḥ", "h", "ā" or whatever, corresponds to a different letter of the Arabic alphabet. There is a one-to-one correlation between the transliterated characters in the Latin script style (the alphabet English-speakers use) and the Arabic letters. Where two Latin-style transliterated characters look similar (as in "ṣ" and "s"), that tells you that (as a non-Arabic-speaker) you will not be very far off the mark if you just go ahead and pronounce the letter as if the dot or line weren't there. Having said this, you can easily improve your pronunciation a bit if you pronounce vowels with lines above them as long vowels (e.g. pronounce *ḥadīth* or hadith as hadeeth).

You may also have noticed the use of the inverted comma (one way round or the other). The mark ' is an Arabic letter called *'ayn*. The mark ' is an Arabic character called *hamza*.[104] Pronounce *hamza* like a glottal stop. (Think of how people from the south east of London such as the actor Michael Caine would pronounce "tt" in the word "bottle".) *'Ayn* is harder to pronounce, with the myriad suggestions from Arabic language experts including the sound that "reproduces the grunt of a camel as it is being loaded" or the sound you make when "you are at the dentist and the drill touches a nerve".[105] One friend suggested to me that you won't go far wrong if you pronounce *'ayn* like a glottal stop too. That is certainly a better suggestion than ignoring the letter.

At this stage, I refer budding Arabic students to Wightwick and Gaafar's *Mastering Arabic* (Palgrave, 2007).

Appendix 1: Study guides

What are these guides?

In conjunction with this book, these guides provide the material for a six-week series entitled "Reaching Muslims: A one-stop course". The series is ideal for pastorates, small groups, community groups or life groups. Including response time, each session takes a little over an hour, so can easily be slotted into an evening programme that also involves coffee, chat, and notices.

Each guide contains the following material: Timings, "The point", Application, Ice-breaker, List of book chapters relevant to the suggested talk and discussion titles, Structured response time (think/pray/do).

How best to use the guides

The leader needs to prepare well. The group members just need to turn up.

The leader should have spent at least two hours reading this book, which is enough time to get through at least half of it.

The members of the group do not need to have had any contact with the book. As long as the leader has prepared using the book and these guides, that will be sufficient to lead group members through the sessions.

Overview of contents

1. What is Islam and who are Muslims? Part 1: Stories and histories, identity, beliefs. Discussion question: Should Christians call God "Allah"?

2. What is Islam and who are Muslims? Part 2: Culture and practices, politics and justice, demographics.

3. Developing open-hearted friendships, Part 1: Why focus on open-hearted friendships? Addressing the fear factor. Cultivate a posture of welcome and acceptance.

4. Developing open-hearted friendships, Part 2: Show by your actions that you welcome and accept Muslims. Level with your Muslim friends.

5. Bible studies to help Muslim friends see Jesus afresh.

6. Discipling believers from a Muslim background. Discussion question: When should a former Muslim who has become a Christian be baptized?

Reaching Muslims Study guide 1:

What is Islam, and who are Muslims? (Part 1)

Timings
5-minute ice-breaker and debrief
25-minute talk
15-minute discussion
25-minute response (discussion and prayer)

The Point
We can have lots of misconceptions about Muslims, but we need to remember that they are people just like us who are friendly, generous, hospitable, hurting, and wonderful. Understanding Muslim worldviews and the diversity of beliefs within Islam will help us to understand Muslims better.

Application
One of the best ways we can come to understand Muslims better is to ask them questions about themselves, their families, their histories and their beliefs. So let's start doing that in our daily lives!

Ice-breaker
Break into groups of two or three and discuss the following:

What words come into your head when someone says "Islam" to you? How do the media portray Muslims?

Talk: What is Islam, and who are Muslims?
In advance, someone in the group should prepare a short talk based on Chapters 1–3.

Discussion: Should Christians call God "Allah"?
Draw on Chapter 25. Other questions:

What are the potential problems with using the word "Allah" for God?

Should Christians use the word "Allah" in situations where it is possible that it might offend other people?

Response

Break into groups and work through the following three sections.

THINK: What one thing have I learnt that has changed my understanding of Islam and Muslims?

PRAY: For God to use your new understanding of Muslim worldviews for his glory.

DO: In twos and threes, discuss one thing that has changed in your thinking after today, and one thing that you want to do practically in response.

Reaching Muslims Study guide 2:

What is Islam, and who are Muslims? (Part 2)

Timings
5-minute ice-breaker and debrief
25-minute talk
15-minute discussion
25-minute response (discussion and prayer)

The Point
A growing awareness of Muslim cultures and worldviews will allow a deepening relationship with Muslim friends. We need to get to know Muslims and the distinctive and related worlds that they inhabit.

Application
Continue to enquire and inform yourself about Muslim culture, and consider how understanding Muslims will enable you to be a better friend to them.

Ice-breaker
Break into groups of two or three and discuss the following:

What do you most admire about Muslim societies?

Talk: What is Islam, and who are Muslims? (Part 2)
In advance, someone in the group should prepare a short talk based on Chapters 4–7.

Discussion: Is it OK for Christians to eat halal meat?
Draw on Chapter 27 to set context.

Questions
Read 1 Corinthians 8:1–13.
What rules does Paul give about eating meat sacrificed to idols?

On what principle are we to decide what we do and don't eat?

Read 1 Corinthians 10:14–31.
How will the questions "Is it helpful?" and "Is it brotherly or sisterly?" affect our attitude to what we eat, and where?

Other material

The instructions of Paul could be summarized as "Do all to God's glory" and "Do nothing to offend". These can help inform our judgment in any given situation. The radical freedom that believers have in Christ goes hand in hand with the law of love that compels them not to do things detrimental to others. (Also see Acts 15:19–29.)

Response

Break into groups and work through the following three sections.

THINK: What practical things do I want to remember for when I meet a Muslim?

PRAY: That God would bring Muslims into your life, for you to befriend.

DO: Commit to one thing that you will do as a result of today.

Reaching Muslims Study guide 3:

Developing open-hearted friendships (Part 1)

Timings
Warning: the timings are tight for this session.

3-minute ice-breaker and debrief
10-minute mini-talk
15-minute discussion and debrief
Another 15-minute mini-talk
20-minute response (discussion and prayer)

The Point
Approach Muslims in friendship and share your lives with them along with the good news about Jesus.

Application
Think about how you could make some Muslim friends, and about how you can welcome these new friends into your life.

Ice-breaker
Break into groups of two or three and discuss the following:

Why is it helpful to be friends with those with whom you are sharing the gospel?

Mini-talk 1: Why focus on open-hearted friendships?
In advance, someone in the group should prepare a very short talk based on Chapter 8.

Discussion: What did Jesus do?

Context

Split into three small groups, each group taking one of the following:

Group 1: John 13: In what ways did Jesus demonstrate sternness and tenderness with Judas? Luke 19: How did Jesus demonstrate friendship with Zacchaeus?

Group 2: Matthew 19:16–22, Matthew 23:13–33, Mark 12:13–17, Luke 7:36–50: What can we learn about how Jesus confronted people, and in what situations?

Group 3: Luke 9:51–56, Luke 10:33–37: Who did Jesus confront, who did he not confront, and why?

Each small group should feed back very briefly to the whole group on Jesus' approach to conversation and confrontation, as well as the specific answers to their questions. That is, three ten-minute small group discussions should happen at the same time. Then five minutes of debrief with the larger group.

Mini-talk 2: Fear and acceptance

Address the fear factor and cultivate a posture of welcome and acceptance

In advance, someone in the group should prepare a very short talk based on Chapters 9 and 10.

Response

Break into groups and brainstorm where you might be able to look to make some Muslim friends. Pray that God would bring them into your life. A structured way to do this is:

THINK: Where could I go in my local neighbourhood to get to know some Muslims?

SAY: One place where you might be able to make some Muslim friends.

PRAY: For God's help in addressing any fears you might have about reaching out to Muslims. Pray that God would bring Muslims into your life.

DO: Give yourself one action point following this week's discussion. Don't use any weasel words in your action point. (Weasel words are words such as "try", "might", or "probably". They help us weasel out of our commitments.[106]) Ask someone else in the group to hold you accountable for fulfilling your commitment.

Reaching Muslims Study guide 4:

Developing open-hearted friendships (Part 2)

Timings
5-minute ice-breaker and debrief
45 minutes for the three-part talk, including a 10-minute activity
25-minute response (discussion and prayer)

The Point
We are best placed to reach Muslim friends when we are wholehearted followers of Jesus ourselves and when we are straight about what we believe and why.

Application
Commit to praying for and engaging with Muslims in your local community.

Ice-breaker
Break into groups of two or three and discuss the following:

What might destroy trust with a Muslim friend?
Give some ideas as to how you could build trust with a Muslim friend.

Talk part 1: Show by your actions that you welcome and accept Muslims
In advance, someone in the group should prepare a very short talk based on Chapter 11. Bear in mind the following quotations:

"In every way… make the teaching about our God and Saviour attractive."

"Trust arrives on foot and leaves on horseback."

Talk part 2: Level with your Muslim friends (part one)

In advance, someone in the group should prepare a very short talk based on the "Invite others into The Story and your story" part of Chapter 12.

Activity

Break into pairs or groups and think about what stories you could tell about your own experience of getting to know God, or about things that he has done in your life. Practise by telling at least part of the story to the person next to you.

Talk part 3: Level with your Muslim friends (part two)

In advance, someone in the group should prepare a very short talk based on the "Prepare to give answers" part of Chapter 12.

Response

Break into groups and work through the following three sections.

THINK: What do I most need to reflect on about the character of God in order to be better equipped to talk about him with Muslim friends?

PRAY: For opportunities to share your story with Muslims in the local community. For wisdom discerning who is genuinely open to finding out more.

DO: Give yourself one action point from today. Ask someone else in the group to hold you accountable.

Reaching Muslims Study guide 5:

This session requires more preparation time for the main leader than do other sessions. It may be worth choosing two people to help lead the Bible studies, briefing them in advance on the need to do some of the preparation.

Timings

5-minute ice-breaker and debrief
5- to 10-minute talk
45-minute Bible study
20-minute response (discussion and prayer)

The Point

The overall story of the Bible and many of the stories within it help Muslims see who Jesus really is. We must learn how to help others appreciate this material.

Application

Get to know how the Bible points people to Jesus.

Ice-breaker

Break into groups of two or three and discuss the following:

How might you use the Bible to help Muslims see Jesus afresh? Be specific.

Mini-talk: Using the Bible to help Muslims see Jesus afresh

Introduction

In advance, someone should prepare a short talk based on the introduction to Part 3 as well as Chapter 17, which includes tips on Bible study with a Muslim.

Discussion: Bible study

Set-up

Split into three groups. Each group should perform a different Bible study for thirty minutes. The purpose of these studies is to sample what it might be like to study the Bible with a Muslim (even though there may well be no Muslims in your group). As you will see, the Bible studies could easily be used in those kind of settings.

The three thirty-minute Bible studies should happen in parallel, which should take thirty minutes in total. The timings are tight, so brief the groups to get started immediately. Everyone should stay in the same room for the studies. It will also help the timings if the leader of each study asks different people to look up each Bible reference before starting the discussion.

After the studies, a spokesperson for each group should feed back what worked well and what could have gone better in their discussion.

Use the material in Chapters 18–20, i.e. the studies on Adam and Eve, Abraham, and Moses. Abbreviated forms of these studies follow below.

ADAM AND EVE: Bible study handout

Context about Islam

Muslims believe that Adam is the first prophet. Adam is mentioned in six *sura*s of the Quran. According to the Quran, Adam and Eve both ate the forbidden fruit and were banished from paradise (heaven) to earth. After they repented on earth, they were forgiven – Muslims do not subscribe to the concept of original sin. Also, some Muslims make a distinction between mistakes and sins. Prophets (according to their view) may make mistakes but are sinless – this includes Adam.

Study together

Read Genesis 3:9–24 together. (You may want to bear in mind Genesis 1:26 – 2:4 and 2:15 – 3:8 as context.)

- What happened to Adam and Eve that day? (They didn't die physically, but they were separated from God.)
- How effective were Adam and Eve's attempts to cover their shame? (Useless.)

Read Mark 10:45 and John 19:16–30 together. Discuss the significance of Jesus' death on the cross in the light of the facts raised earlier. Recall from Genesis that death means separation from God, who is our source of life. Discuss the link with shame and honour: Jesus' death sets us free from shame.

Read Romans 5:14–15 and 6:23 together.
- Did Jesus sin?
- Did God need to penalize Jesus as he did Adam and Eve?
- Note that in Romans 5–6 another free gift – a greater one, eternal life – is on offer from God.

Abraham: A Bible study handout

Context about Islam

Abraham is known as the friend of God in Islam. His name appears sixty-nine times in the Quran. Following in the footsteps of Abraham is very important to Muslims. Muslims believe that the son Abraham offered up for sacrifice was Ishmael, not Isaac. In what follows, I recommend not making much of this difference in views between Muslims and Christians. More important is to make the point that a sacrifice was needed and that God provided it.

Study

Read Genesis 12:1–3 together. (Before this, the world was full of false ideas and confusion – Genesis 11, Babel.) What was God's plan to deal with this situation?

Read Genesis 15:1–6 and 17:1–8 together. Context: Abram had become too old to have a child. The reason for Abram/Abraham's name change is in 17:5 – it was to reaffirm the covenant God made.

- What did God promise Abram?
- What was Abram's response, and on what basis did God count him righteous?
- If you have time, look at Genesis 22:1–14, noting the significance of Abraham's obedience there.

Now read Romans 4:1–5 and John 3:16 together. According to this, on what basis can someone get right with God? (Other useful context here, depending on how the discussion goes, is Mark 15:22 – 16:8 and John 1:12.)

Other relevant Bible passages on Abraham include James 2:23 (Abraham as the friend of God) and Galatians 3:6–9 (Abraham and the importance of faith).

Moses: A Bible study handout

Context about Islam

The name of Moses is the most frequently occurring of all the Islamic prophets in the Quran. The Quran teaches that Allah spoke directly to Moses (something not said of Muhammad). Muslims think that Moses' life and work as a messenger, lawgiver, and leader most closely foreshadows that of Muhammad.

Study

Read Exodus 12:1–6 and 21–27 together.

- Background to bear in mind: previous slavery in Egypt, God's raising up of Moses, the plagues, and the deliverance of God's people. Note that God put in place a sacrifice system (verses 6 and 21).
- What kind of sacrifice was it?
- What did the sacrifice involve?
- What kind of animal needed to be slaughtered?

Read John 1:29. Note that by now, the above sacrifice system (to get right with God) had been in operation for the 1,500 years leading up to and including the time of Jesus. That is, God's people were frequently reminded of a lamb that had died in their place. What did John the Baptist call Jesus?

Read 1 Peter 1:17–20. What similarities are there between this description and the story from Exodus?

Depending on what point the discussion has reached, you may need to make the connection between our sins, the need for sacrifice, and Jesus' provision of that sacrifice. Perhaps use Romans 3:21–26.

Response

Break into groups and work through the following three sections.

THINK: Which of the Bible studies resonated most with you, and why?

PRAY: For Muslims to develop a hunger for the Bible. For you to understand it better.

DO: Set yourself a specific and manageable goal in terms of improving your understanding of the Bible.

Reaching Muslims Study guide 6:

Discipling believers from a Muslim background

Timings
5-minute ice-breaker and debrief
10-minute talk
25-minute discussion, including 5- to 10-minute talk to set the context at the start
20-minute response (discussion and prayer) – if possible add in some extra time to cover other issues that have come up during the whole series

The Point
Discipling new Christians is a vital task, including if they were formerly Muslims. We must give ourselves to this task.

Application
Community needs to be in the DNA of our church. Let's make sure we contribute to this.

Ice-breaker
Break into groups of two or three and discuss the following:

What problems might you face if you migrated to a new country? How would you most like to be supported?

Talk: Discipling former Muslims who have come to follow Jesus
In advance, have someone prepare a short talk based on Chapter 13. Remember: for some, starting to follow Jesus is like migrating to a new country.

When should a former Muslim who has become a Christian be baptized?

In advance, have someone prepare a short talk based on Chapter 26.

Discussion

What factors do you think are most important in guiding when a Muslim background believer should be baptized?

What if you suspect that an asylum seeker is using baptism as a passport to citizenship? (This has happened in some churches in the UK in recent years.)

Response

Break into groups and work through the following sections.

THINK: What do I need to do to help our church become ready to receive Muslims who decide to follow Jesus? How available am I to my Muslim friends, or friends generally?

PRAY: For Muslims to come to appreciate Jesus for who he is. For Muslims to take steps of faith to follow him.

DO: Review your action points from earlier sessions. Set one final action point: one thing that you will do as a result of these six sessions.

Appendix 2: Useful resources

The star ratings in the key denote increasing levels of difficulty, not how good I think any given resource is.

> ## Key
>
> * very accessible to all
> ** fairly accessible
> *** academic
> [C] Explicitly Christian perspective
> [M] Explicitly Muslim perspective

Apologetics

From a Muslim point of view

** Rahmatullah Kairanvi, M., *Izhar-ul-haq (The Truth Revealed),* London: Ta-Ha Publishers Ltd, 2003. Attempts to show that the Bible cannot be a revealed book and to refute the doctrine of the Trinity. Refers to various scriptures and Muslim and Christian scholars. [M] 474 pages.

** Islamic web: www.islamicweb.com – presented in a style that seems quite close to that of some Christian evangelistic sites. [M].

From a Christian point of view

** Coplestone, F. S., *Jesus Christ or Mohammed? A guide to Islam and Christianity that helps explain the differences,* Fern: Christian Focus Publications, 2000. Characteristically thought-provoking, bite-sized treatment of seventeen key issues. [C] 160 pages.

** Pfander, C. G., *The Mizan-ul-haqq (Balance of Truth),* Villach: Light of

Life, 1986. Polemic work on revelation, including defence of the Bible and questioning whether Islam is God's final revelation. [C] 370 pages.

* Rhodes, R., *The 10 Things You Need to Know About Islam*, Oregon: Harvest House Publishers, 2007. Has "Do you want direct answers to your questions about Muslims?" in big letters on the back cover. Also contains some helpfully brief content on common questions. [C] 155 pages.

** Zwemer, S. M., *Islam and the Cross: Selections from "The Apostle to Islam"*, edited by Roger S. Greenway, New Jersey: P&R Publishing, 2002. Presents Christianity in context of Muslim beliefs. Quite polemic and very respectful. [C] 165 pages.

** Debate.org: www.debate.org.uk – wide range of polemic and apologetic articles on theological, social, and other questions. [C].

** Answering Islam: www.answering-Islam.org – evangelical site aiming at "Christian–Muslim dialogue". [C].

Islam – history, doctrine, and practices

History

** Afsaruddin, A., *The First Muslims: History and Memory*, Oxford: Oneworld, 2008. Reconstruction of the first three centuries of Islam from a largely traditional Muslim perspective. [M] 254 pages.

** Cleveland, W. L., *A History of the Modern Middle East* (third edition), Oxford: Westview Press, 2004. Very well written and mainly focused on the last 220 years. 588 pages.

** Cook, D., *Understanding Jihad*, Berkeley: University of California Press, 2005. The seminal study in its field. 259 pages.

* Cook, M., *Muhammad*, Oxford: Oxford University Press, 1996. Excellent, very readable work by a renowned scholar. 94 pages.

* Hourani, A., *A History of the Arab Peoples*, London: Faber and Faber, 2005. Deservedly a classic, covering from pre-Islamic times until just after AD 2000. 566 pages.

*** Humphreys, R. S., *Islamic History: A Framework for Inquiry*, Princeton: Princeton University Press, 1991. Technical, scholarly work with an excellent section on sources and research tools. 401 pages.

Quran

** Jones, A., *The Qur'ān,* Exeter: Short Run Press, 2007. An excellent translation of the Quran from a Western scholarly perspective, with a good introduction. 605 pages.

** Parrinder, G., *Jesus in the Qur'ān*, Oxford: Oneworld, 2003. Thought-provoking. 187 pages.

** Robinson, N., *Discovering the Qur'ān: A Contemporary Approach to a Veiled Text,* London: SCM Press, 2003. Very sympathetic to traditional Muslim interpretations on some issues. A very useful introduction to issues of dating and chronology in the suras. 332 pages.

** Abdullah Yusuf Ali, *The Holy Qur'ān,* London: Albirr Foundation, 2004. Translation of the Quran, with commentary from a traditional Muslim perspective. [M] 1,761 pages.

Doctrine and practices

*** Burton, J., *An Introduction to the Hadith*, Edinburgh: Edinburgh University Press, 2001. Dense and authoritative. 210 pages.

** Ernst, C. W., *The Shambhala Guide to Sufism*, Boston: Shambhala Publications, 1997. Very readable historical and contemporary introduction to the philosophy and practice of Sufism. 264 pages.

** Hewer, C. T. R., *Understanding Islam: The First Ten Steps*, London: SCM Press, 2008. A more in-depth introduction to some of the maps presented in Part I of this book, especially beliefs and practices. Written by a Christian and praised on the back cover by the Muslim Yahya Michot as being "authentic to our tradition". [C] 244 pages.

** Moucarry, C., *The Search for Forgiveness: Pardon and Punishment in Islam and Christianity,* Leicester: Inter-Varsity Press, 2004. Explores answers Islam gives to questions of pardon, punishment, reconciliation, and many others. [C] 374 pages.

* Sookhdeo, P., *A Christian's Pocket Guide to Islam*, Pewsey: Isaac Publishing, 2001. Clearly written and focusing on the history and beliefs of Muslims. [C] 111 pages.

** Taha, M. M., *The Second Message of Islam*, Syracuse: Syracuse University Press, 1987. Controversial alternative reading of Islam by the prominent Sudanese Muslim teacher executed by the Sudanese government in 1985. [M] 178 pages.

** Vikør, K. S., *Between God and the Sultan: A History of Islamic Law*, London: Hurst and Company, 2005. Covers the theory, application, and history of Islamic law, including *shari'a* and the four schools. 387 pages.

** The Council of ex-Muslims of Britain: www.ex-Muslim.org.uk – "Non-believers, atheists and ex-Muslims", affiliated to the British Humanist Association.

* Islam Guide: www.Islam-guide.com – "For non-Muslims who would like to understand Islam, Muslims (Moslems), and the Holy Quran (Koran)." [M].

* Islam Q&A: www.Islam-qa.com – "Responses are composed by Sheikh Muhammed Salih Al-Munajjid, a known Islamic lecturer and author." [M].

Islam – relationships and journeys

Relating to Muslims

* Adeney, M., *Daughters of Islam: Building Bridges with Muslim Women,* Leicester: Inter-Varsity Press, 2002. Strategies for relating to Muslim women where you are. [C] 224 pages.

* Bell, S., *Grace for Muslims? The Journey from Fear to Faith*, Milton Keynes: Authentic, 2008. "A grace response" is the crucial ingredient Bell advocates in our relations with Muslims. See especially pp. 126–30 (stories of Jesus appearing to Muslims – subtitled "Beware, God is at work") and Chapter 7 (The Local Church as a Receiving Centre). [C] 190 pages.

** Chapman, C., *Cross and Crescent: Responding to the Challenge of Islam,* Leicester, Inter-Varsity Press, 1999. Covers the basics of Islam including using discussion and dialogue effectively. Robust and irenic. [C] 346 pages.

* Cooper, A. and Maxwell, E. A. (eds.), *Ishmael My Brother: A Christian Introduction to Islam,* Oxford: Monarch, 2003. Excellent introduction to Islamic beliefs, practices, culture, history, and political developments. [C] 352 pages.

** Musk, B., *Touching the Soul of Islam: Sharing the Gospel in Muslim Cultures,* Oxford: Monarch, 2004. Excellent on cross-cultural issues, including helping understand themes in tension such as honour/shame, hospitality/violence, and brotherhood/rivalry. [C] 317 pages.

** Musk, B., *Kissing Cousins? Christians and Muslims Face to Face,* Oxford: Monarch, 2005. Very good at seeking common ground. [C] 480 pages.

* Stacey, V., *Meeting Muslims: Practical Lessons,* Manila: OMF Literature, 2006. Practical steps, taking into account culture, language, practices and important sensitivities. [C] 80 pages.

Stories of changes in faith perspective

* Brother Andrew and Janssen, A., *Secret Believers: What Happens When Muslims Believe in Christ,* London: Hodder, 2007. A novel, presenting true stories of Muslims who have become Christians. [C] 276 pages.

* Husain, E., *The Islamist,* London: Penguin Books, 2007. Much quoted, gripping bestseller by a former radical British Muslim, now a moderate Muslim. [M] 288 pages.

* Orr-Ewing, F. and A., *Holy Warriors: A Fresh Look at the Face of Extreme Islam,* Cumbria: Authentic, 2003. Excellent work not just because of the story of the authors meeting the Taliban, but also because of the short introduction to Islam and avenues for Christian responses. [C] 117 pages.

* Shah, H. *The Imam's Daughter*, London: Rider, 2010.

* Sheikh, B., *I Dared to Call Him Father: The Miraculous Story of a Muslim Woman's Encounter with God,* Eastbourne: Kingsway, 2003. Jesus appears to a high-born Muslim Pakistani woman. New edition with previously unpublished material which brings the story up to date. [C] 190 pages.

* Zeidan, D., *The Fifth Pillar: A Spiritual Pilgrimage,* Carlisle: OM Publishing, 1993. An educated young Arab Muslim discovers Jesus. [C] 143 pages.

Islam – socio-political and demographic issues

Politics and ideology

** Kepel, G., *Allah in the West: Islamic Movements in America and Europe,* Cambridge: Polity Press, 2004. Analysis of Islamic movements in America, Britain and France. 273 pages.

* Phillips, M., *Londonistan: How Britain is Creating a Terror State Within,* London: Gibson Square, 2006. Much quoted provocative bestseller. 336 pages.

*** Ye'or, B., *Eurabia: The Euro–Arab Axis,* Madison: Fairleigh Dickinson University Press, 2006. Cerebral book by an Egyptian-born author on the posited transformation of Europe into a cultural and political appendage of the Arab/Muslim world. 384 pages.

Demographics

** Esposito, J. and Mogahed, D., *Who Speaks for Islam? What a Billion Muslims Really Think,* New York: Gallup Press, 2007. The product of a six-year Gallup World Poll research study based on tens of thousands of thirty- to sixty-minute interviews with a sample of Muslims representing 90 per cent of the world's Muslims. 204 pages.

* Lewis, P., *Young, British and Muslim,* London: Continuum, 2007. Pithy examination of the lives and beliefs of British Muslims aged 18–30. 160 pages.

** Riddell, P., *Christians and Muslims: Pressures and Potential in a Post-9/11 World,* Leicester: Inter-Varsity Press, 2004. Discussion of diverse Muslim approaches to British society, as well as how Christians are responding and what more can be done. [C] 254 pages.

Organizations

** Council on American–Islamic Relations (CAIR): www.cair.com. Claims to be America's largest civil liberties organization, aiming "to enhance understanding of Islam". Has been heavily criticized (and has made responses to those criticisms) in relation to purported funding links with Hamas.

* Muslim Council of Britain: www.mcb.org.uk – claims to be a UK "national representative Muslim umbrella body". [M].

** Jihad watch: www.jihadwatch.org – tracks and reports instances of jihad globally.

** International Institute for Islamic Thought: www.iiituk.com and www.iiit.org – dedicated to the "reform and revival of Islamic thought" (mainly USA-focused). [M].

Other resources

** Bailey, K. E., *Jesus Through Middle Eastern Eyes: Cultural Studies in the Gospels*, London: SPCK, 2008. Deep understanding of Middle Eastern culture insightfully brought to bear on some New Testament parables (including many from Luke), with unmatched skill. [C] 400 pages.

** Frisby, M., *Reaching the Nations: Recommendations for Local Church Leaders*, Brighton: Newfrontiers, 2005. Practical guide containing suggestions to help those who may be called to plant churches in non-Western countries. [C] 68 pages.

** Love, R., *Muslims, Magic and the Kingdom of God: Church Planting Among Folk Muslims,* Pasadena: William Carey Library, 2000. Focused on church planting among folk Muslims. [C] 252 pages.

*** Wright, C., *The Mission of God: Unlocking the Bible's Grand Narrative*, Nottingham: IVP, 2006. Masterful in its explanation of the flow of revelation from the Old to New Testament. [C] 581 pages.

* www.Islam-guide.com/frm-ch3-2.htm: A good introduction to Islamic beliefs. [M]

* BBC website: www.bbc.co.uk/religion – follow the link to Islam – some good background material.

Appendix 3: Further guidance for preachers: Use stories and be mindful of non-Western perspectives

(Note: If you are not a preacher, this section could still be relevant to you in terms of how you explain aspects of Christianity to others. It overlaps with the section entitled "Invite others into The Story and your story" in Chapter 12.)

In your sermon preparation, try reading the Bible from a non-Western perspective. Of course, West-friendly application is important. But in mining the original meaning of the text, remember that Christianity is an Eastern religion. The Bible is saturated with material emphasizing the cultural importance of factors such as honour (over freedom from guilt), family (over career),[107] and hospitality (over "get it yourself"), things that matter a lot to those of African, Asian, and Middle Eastern origin. Works such as the *Africa Bible Commentary* or Kenneth E. Bailey's *Jesus Through Middle Eastern Eyes* are invaluable tools, but no substitute for the rewarding work of understanding the original context of the Bible yourself. Understanding this original context is an excellent thing to do, not just because the situations of many Bible characters are very close to those faced by many Muslims today, but also because – for everybody – a sermon with good exegesis is a good sermon.

Also, storytelling is central not just to non-Western cultures, but also to the Islamic religious heritage.[108] So tell stories in your preaching. Beyond this, remember: is there really anyone who does not love a good story? Even if Western cultures sometimes involve more propositional than narrative forms of communication, story is also central for us. I have never heard a great preacher who is not a great storyteller. And contrary to what some think, deep down we are all naturals; we just have to learn how to tell the story "our way". Similarly, resist the urge to turn a biblical story into a set of propositions. Often, the story will illustrate itself. Think hard: why are you toying with a biblical narrative? I suggest that you need very good reason if you are going to do this. To finish this storytelling paragraph, a dangerous thought: rather than just using a couple of stories here and there to spice things up, or as icing on the cake as a point of application, experiment with "story" being the fundamental structural principle of your sermon. In this way, you risk unleashing the captivating power of story more fully. Eugene Lowry will show you the way.[109] I think that neither you nor your listeners will be disappointed by such an attempt.

The above two pieces of advice will help generate open hearts among many Muslims, because of the cultural connections you will make through not being excessively wedded to Western and propositional approaches. Maybe you require practical tips on how to preach effective sermons to Muslims (or audiences containing some Muslims and some others). My preaching style is unlikely to be very similar to yours, so there is a limit to how far my preferences and advice will be directly applicable to you. However, you may find some of the outlines in Part 3 useful as a starting point. Part 3 also contains some Bible study outlines, which may be modified for use in sermons.

Appendix 4: Further guidance for church leaders: Decide the level of priority that Muslim outreach has and will have in your church

Any truly vibrant church will be sharing Jesus with those around them, whether those people are Muslims or non-Muslims. Equally, individuals in your church may take particular initiative to learn about and connect with Muslims they know. This is different from the question of the extent to which your church is strategically, systematically planning to reach out to Muslims.

My goal here is not to persuade leadership teams of churches to go for any particular strategy, or for others to lobby for particular approaches. For some, reaching Muslims will be strategically important. For others it will be less so, and that is fine. A church's geographical location and stage of development are related to why it may or may not decide to focus (at a particular point in time) on Muslim outreach.

The key here is: set priorities, or others will set them for you. This is especially important in respect of Muslim outreach, because of the high profile and often impassioned nature of coverage about Islam. In the absence of clearly set and clearly communicated priorities, your leadership agenda could be derailed by a group of well meaning, mission-minded yet poorly directed members of your church who are focused on the vast need and opportunity in relation to Muslim outreach. Maybe the derailing is of God, maybe not. All the more reason to be explicit in your praying and planning about this. Also, even if reaching out to Muslims is not a strategic priority for your church, make sure you identify those in your number who do have a particular passion for this. Pray for them and support them in other ways.

The point that follows may surprise you: if you decide as a leadership team not to set Muslim outreach as a priority, simply having an explicit discussion within your leadership team may help others connect with Muslims. For example, one thing you may say to those with Muslim friends after the leadership discussion has taken place is, "Reaching those Muslims is vital for us, not as part of our church-wide strategic goals, but as part of what we must all individually continue to do – namely, to be contagious for Jesus in all parts of our lives." In this way you help remove any sense which could otherwise arise, that you as a leadership team do not value others spending time with, and/or reaching out to, Muslims. So, try putting this on your next leadership meeting agenda: "Where does reaching Muslims fit on our medium- and long-term priority list for us as a church?" Discussing this and agreeing actions may help clarify your next steps as a church in surprising ways.

Whatever you decide, take seriously your wider responsibility to reach Muslims in the Muslim world. Think through how you can guide people towards exploring involvement in church planting in the 10–40 window where appropriate. A good resource to guide you in this is *Reaching the Nations: Recommendations for Local Church Leaders* by Mike Frisby.[110]

Finally, as you decide what sort of approach to pursue, remember that leaders are not immune from the fears outlined in Chapter 9. Those fears can lead to all sorts of unhelpful leadership behaviours. Some leaders effectively lash out, whether in sermons or in private conversations, attacking Islam without a sound knowledge base and showing little consideration or respect. Others ask the "specialists" to do the work of engaging with Muslims. Still others do nothing, paralysed by despair at the size and complexity of the task. None of these fight, flight, or freeze responses are helpful, and all are contagious to those we lead.

Notes

1. Unsourced quotations are taken from things I have heard personally.

2. This sentence was affirmed by the majority of respondents to a Gallup Poll in countries with sizeable Muslim populations (Esposito, J. and Mogahed, D., *Who Speaks for Islam? What a Billion Muslims Really Think*, New York: Gallup Press, 2007, p. 22).

3. From Alam, M. Y. (ed.), *Made in Bradford*, cited in Lewis, P., *Young, British and Muslim*, London: Continuum, 2007, p. 1.

4. Eid al-Fitr is the Muslim holiday or festival at the end of the Islamic month of fasting, Ramadan. Eid al-Adha is another festival, linked to the rites of the Mecca pilgrimage (see Chapter 3) and commemorating Abraham's willingness to sacrifice his son.

5. This feature of stories is why many of the above stories overlap.

6. See Chapter 3 for more information about the Quran.

7. See "al-Ḳuds", an article by Goitein and Grabar in the *Encyclopedia of Islam* (second edition), vol. 5, pp. 322ff.

8. See http://www.census.gov/compendia/statab/cats/population/religion. html (accessed 3 January 2010).

9. Nominal Muslims are those who are Muslims by background and/or culture, but who do not observe many of the stipulations of the faith.

10. I heard him say this first-hand when he was addressing a local community meeting in Oxford (UK) in 2007.

11. Muslims differ over the terminology applied to a Muslim who lacks such beliefs. Examples include "apostate", "not a Muslim any more" or "not a good Muslim".

12. From *Good News for Muslims* (Global Connections, www. globalconnections.co.uk). Used with permission. Similar statements may be found in Islamic sources, including *The Muslim Directory* (UK, AD 2008/09, 1429/30 AH, pp. 485–6) and www.islamicweb.com.

13. See, for example, "Muṣḥaf", an article by Harald Motzki in the *Encyclopedia of the Qur'ān* (vol. 3, p. 463).

14. Muslim schools of law are primarily "fully parallel legal systems, each with their own methodology and rules; most often with separate courts and judges" (Vikør, K. S., *Between God and the Sultan: A History of Islamic Law*, London: Hurst and Company, 2005, p. 10).

15. Muslims often associate their beliefs that Jesus was not crucified and that someone substituted the body with the verse Q4:157. (This coding refers to the 157th *aya* in the fourth *sura* of the Quran.) By contrast, Ahmadiyya Muslims believe that Jesus survived crucifixion and travelled to India to continue his ministry among the lost tribes of Israel. Founded at the end of the nineteenth century, the Ahmadiyya movement considers itself Muslim, but most Muslims consider it heretical. The Ahmadiyyas are a relatively small group and very active in reaching out to non-Muslims. For Ahmadiyya views on Jesus, see http://www.alislam.org/topics/jesus/index.php (accessed 23 November 2009).

16. Shi'i and Sunni Muslims number approximately 10% and 85% respectively of all Muslims worldwide.

17. Sufism is a difficult aspect of Islam to define and tends to relate to Islam's mystical or ascetic dimensions. Wahhabism originated in the eighteenth century with a programme of bringing Islam back to its roots by weeding out things that were seen as innovations that had crept into Islam since early times. Salafi Wahhabism, a particularly extreme form that tries to insist on only observing practices that were known in the time of Muhammad and the first three generations of his followers, has become influential in Saudi Arabia.

18. The publication of Rushdie's *Satanic Verses* in 1988 led to violent protests, with Ayatollah Khomeini (Supreme Leader of Iran) issuing a fatwa against Rushdie in February 1989. For discussion about the bounty element of the fatwa, see http://answering-ansar.org/answers/bidah/bidah.pdf (accessed 7 June 2010).

19. *Muslim Americans: Middle Class and Mostly Mainstream*, a report by the Pew Research Center, May 2007, http://pewresearch.org/assets/pdf/Muslim-americans.pdf, accessed 3 January 2010. The report was based on interviews with 1,050 Muslim American adults, conducted between January and April 2007. Hereafter referred to as *Muslim Americans*.

20. From a Channel 4 survey as part of the Dispatches programme "Muslim Attitudes to Living in Britain", first broadcast on 27 April 2006 (cited in Lewis, P., *Young, British and Muslim*, 2007, p. 11). Contrary to the claims of some, Islamic premodern sources do not associate jihad primarily with an internal, non-violent spiritual struggle rather than an external militaristic one. While these sources do position jihad as a devotional, spiritual struggle, this is almost always (and in the earliest sources) inseparable from the militaristic kind. For more on this, see Chatrath, N. (2010), "Fighting the unbeliever: Anjem Choudary, Musharraf Hussain and pre-modern sources on Sura 9:29, abrogation and Jihad", in *Islam and Christian-Muslim Relations*, 21: 2, 111–126.

21. http://www.wnd.com/news/article.asp?ARTICLE_ID=34223 (accessed 16 February 2010).

22. http://www.mcb.org.uk/media/pr/110901.htm (accessed 22 February 2007).

23. Esposito, J. and Mogahed, D., *Who Speaks for Islam?*, 2007, p. 1.

24. For more examples and discussion of Muslim cultures and practices see Musk, B., *Touching the Soul of Islam: Sharing the Gospel in Muslim Cultures*, Oxford: Monarch, 2004 and Hewer, C. T. R., *Understanding Islam: The First Ten Steps*, London: SCM Press, 2008 respectively.

25. In November 2009, the Malaysian Government "refused to release 10,000 Bibles which it seized because they contained the word Allah to refer to God" (http://news.bbc.co.uk/1/hi/world/asia-pacific/8343626.stm, accessed 25 October 2010). Roughly two-thirds of Malaysia's population is Muslim and, in December 2009, the Malaysian High Court ruled that Christians have a constitutional right to use the word "Allah" to refer to God (http://news.bbc.co.uk/1/hi/world/asia-pacific/8435975.stm, accessed 3 January 2010). Among other things, this controversy raises a terminological question, dealt with in Chapter 25: What is the scope of the word "Allah"?

26. Do not assume that individuals wearing head coverings will necessarily use any of these three words to describe what they are wearing. The term *hijab* is sometimes used as a generic word for any kind of head covering (including the *niqab*, *burqa* and other types of covering) and the terms *niqab* and *burqa* are sometimes used interchangeably.

27. The main Quranic command about this is given in *sura* 24:30–31.

28. *Muslim Americans*, p. 47. Among US Muslims, liberals marginally outnumber conservatives, whereas in the general US public conservatives outnumber liberals by almost two to one ("liberal" and "conservative" as defined in the report cited).

29. This illustrates some of the impact that major events and policies have on Muslim voters. See http://www.allied-media.com/AM/poltical. htm [sic.] (a group of three surveys that the author of the site calls "unscientific") and *Muslim Americans*, p. 47.

30. Many Muslims have become involved in the West in positively making a difference in the law and politics, for example as judges and elected representatives. But some extremist Muslims denounce such involvement as not reflecting Islamic codes of conduct.

31. The Muslim Council of Britain (MCB) illustrates the way in which attempts to set up umbrella bodies for Muslims have met with criticism from Muslims. See, for example, the views of Abdul Rehman-Malik, contributing editor of the Muslim magazine *Q-News*, at http://mcbwatch.blogspot.com/2005/08/self-criticism-is-for-wimps.html (accessed 27 November 2009).

32. In the UK recent polls have shown 40–60% of Muslims in favour of *shari'a* courts, although some have disputed the way the questions have been put in many of these polls. The number of *shari'a* courts currently sitting in the UK is probably significantly less than the 80–85 sometimes reported in the press, unless one includes examples of individual imams giving advice in a mosque. See http://www.dailymail.co.uk/news/article-1196165/Britain-85-sharia-courts-The-astonishing-spread-Islamic-justice-closed-doors.html (accessed 27 November 2009). To compare the different views of extremist and moderate Muslims on *shari'a*, see Riddell, P., *Christians and Muslims: Pressures and Potential in a Post-9/11 World*, Leicester: Inter-Varsity Press, 2004, pp. 64, 78.

33. In the USA, nearly two-thirds of Muslims believe that a Muslim may marry a non-Muslim (see *Muslim Americans*, p. 40 – 70% of Muslim men and 54% of Muslim women hold this belief). Muslims differ over whether such marriages are legally valid within Islam. Q2:221 is an important verse in this context.

34. These issues are faced head-on in the article "Radical Islam in Europe"

by Leslie Lebl (*Orbis*, Jan. 2010, vol. 54, issue 1, pp. 46–60).

35. Although illustrated here in relation to the UK, this trend has relevance elsewhere. There are also echoes of the second of the "My parents just don't get it" stories in Part 1 ("Stories and histories").

36. *Mapping the Global Muslim Population*, the Pew Forum, 2009, p. 4 (see www.pewforum.org, accessed 8 October 2009). This study of more than 200 countries estimated that there were 1.57 billion Muslims in the world in 2009, or 23% of the global population. Hereafter referred to as *Mapping the Global Muslim Population*.

37. The main source for this table is *Mapping the Global Muslim Population* (see above note). The Muslim populations given in relation to Germany, France, and the Netherlands account for 5–6% of the total populations of those countries. In the UK the figure is 3–4% of the population. In the USA, Canada, Australia, and South Africa, Muslims represent less than 2% of the total populations.

38. The population of Muslims in non-Muslim countries is the topic of seemingly endless debate. Estimates of the size of the US Muslim population range from 1.3 million to 6–7 million. The sources for these figures are, respectively, the "American Religious Identification Survey", a report by Barry Kosmin and Ariela Keysar of Trinity College, Connecticut, based on a survey carried out during February–November 2008 (http://livinginliminality.files.wordpress.com/2009/03/aris_report_2008.pdf, accessed 3 January 2010) and "The Mosque in America: A National Portrait", a report of the Council on American-Islamic Relations based on a 2000 mosque study project (http://www.cair.com/AmericanMuslims/ReportsandSurveys.aspx, accessed 3 January 2010).

39. Excluding Russia.

40. Thirty per cent of adult Muslims in the USA are between the ages of 18 and 29 compared with 21% for the general US population, and 13% are over the age of 54 compared with 30% for the general US population. Home-owning percentages are 41% for US Muslims compared with 68% for the general population. Data drawn from *Muslim Americans* (see above for reference). In relation to the statistics about home ownership, this source does not state whether it (or its own source) corrected for differences in household size.

41. Comparing the population of Muslims to the general population, based on *Muslim Americans*, percentage income disparities seem to be higher in France, Spain, Germany, and Great Britain than in the USA, although it is difficult to be certain because the income ranges were not exactly comparable.

42. TUC report, 2005, cited in http://news.bbc.co.uk/1/hi/uk/4177116. stm (accessed 23 November 2009); "Religion in Prison", http://www. hmprisonservice.gov.uk/resourcecentre/prisonservicejournal/index. asp?id=4864,3124,11,3148,0,0 (accessed 23 November 2009). For more information on UK Muslim demographics, see "Britain's Muslim Communities: A Sketch", a chapter in Lewis, P., *Young, British and Muslim*.

43. *Muslim Americans* (see reference above).

44. Especially among economic migrants, there is an increasing number of Muslims coming from Kosovo, Albania, and other areas of Eastern Europe to the UK.

45. Inspector Morse is a fictional Oxford-based detective created by the author Colin Dexter.

46. An additional example is John 3, where Jesus is recorded as having used both dialogue and confrontation in the one conversation with Nicodemus. We must of course think through where to draw the line between the actions of Jesus (who had a particular, once-for-all mission) and our actions. But we must not forget that Jesus' example is our best model.

47. For a variety of examples and advice, see Acts 13:46; 17:4; 18:6; 18:28; 19:8–9; Romans 2:4; 2 Corinthians 5:11 (persuading in the context of reconciliation) and 2 Timothy 2:2.

48. Crist, T. M., *Learning the Language of Babylon*, Grand Rapids: Chosen Books, 2001, p. 154.

49. The story in this paragraph is told in Crist, T. M., *Learning the Language of Babylon*.

50. For more stories, see also www.muslimjourneytohope.com, Shah, H., *The Imam's Daughter*, London: Rider, 2010 and Bell, S., *Grace for Muslims? The Journey from Fear to Faith*, Milton Keynes: Authentic, 2008 (especially pp. 126–30).

51. Because this is different from our Gregorian, solar calendar, the Islamic month of Ramadan falls during a different Gregorian month each year. (Twenty seconds on Google will tell you when Ramadan is in any given year.)

52. Ida Glaser assembled this fictional scenario from a large number of real situations with which she has been involved. The names have been changed.

53. Dr F. Goodsell, quoted in Zwemer, S. M., *Islam and the Cross: Selections from "The Apostle to Islam"*, edited by Roger S. Greenway, New Jersey: P&R Publishing, 2002, p. 55.

54. Google "Islamic calendar" to find out the right dates for the start of the Islamic year.

55. Leonard Sweet, cited in Crist, T. M., *Learning the Language of Babylon*, p. 143.

56. Stacey, V., *Meeting Muslims: Practical Lessons*, Manila: OMF Literature, 2006, pp. 14–15. Many mosques have signs reminding worshippers only to enter the main hall if they have the "right intention". So some Muslims might doubt how meritorious the actions of the first man in the above example really were. Nevertheless, it is a helpful parable.

57. For variations on this theme, see the series of parables suggested for use with Muslim enquirers in Stacey, V., *Meeting Muslims*, pp. 16–17.

58. For a well sourced explanation of the lack of evidence that early Muslims believed the Bible to be corrupted, see www.answering-islam. org/authors/adams/early_islam_bible.html (accessed 18 February 2010).

59. Mark 16:9–20 and John 7:53 – 8:11.

60. Edward Evans, from an email I have seen.

61. *Voices from Christians in Britain with a Muslim background: Stories for the British church on evangelism, conversion, integration and discipleship*, an MA dissertation by Thomas J. Walsh, Birmingham Christian College, 2005 (used with permission). For a copy of the dissertation, contact tomandjudi@blueyonder.co.uk.

62. From *Voices from Christians in Britain with a Muslim Background* (see note above).

63. Edward Evans, from an email I have seen.

64. Some of the material in the rest of this paragraph is drawn from "Interludes", sections within Musk, B., 2005.

65. Acts 2:1–11. The record of the apostle Peter's speech makes clear Luke's approval.

66. Galatians 1:17–18.

67. Parrinder, G., *Jesus in the Qur'ān*, Oxford: Oneworld, 2003, p. 16. The Quran translations are from the Alan Jones version.

68. See for example the survey by Zwemer, S., *Islam and the Cross*, pp. 10–16.

69. From *sura* 10:94, Alan Jones translation. The Quran sometimes refers to Allah as "I" and sometimes as "We". This latter usage does not mean that Muslims believe that God is in any sense plural.

70. Yusuf Ali provides no reason for his assertion that the Scripture before Muhammad includes Islamic revelation as well as pre-Islamic revelation (Abdullah Yusuf Ali, *The Holy Qur'ān*, London: Albirr Foundation, p. 504).

71. It also differs from how Orthodox, Catholic, or Protestant Christians would describe Christianity today. For example, Mary is perceived as one of three Christian gods, as in *sura* 5:116, "And behold! Allah will say: 'O Jesus the son of Mary! Didst thou say unto men, worship me and my mother as gods in derogation of Allah?'"

72. See Q6:114–5.

73. Parrinder, G., *Jesus in the Qur'ān*, p. 168.

74. Wright, N. T., *The Challenge of Jesus*, London: SPCK, 2000, pp. 20–21.

75. Moucarry, C., *The Search for Forgiveness: Pardon and Punishment in Islam and Christianity*, Leicester: Inter-Varsity Press, 2004, pp. 168–9.

76. Bannister, A., *The Quest for the Lost Jesus*, www.answering-Islam.org/

Andy/quest1.html (accessed 14 January 2010).

77. Acts 17:30–31; compare with Matthew 16:27; 25:31–33; John 5:27; Acts 10:42; Romans 2:16.

78. Alternatively you may want to modify these outlines for use as the basis for a talk or as an introduction to a small group Bible study.

79. If your friend raises the objection that Moses is a forerunner of Muhammad rather than of Jesus, consult the tract "Is there a prediction of Muhammad in the Taurat?", www.debate.org.uk/topics/trtracts/t03. htm (accessed 6 June 2010).

80. This outline is based on material given to me by Martin Whittingham, used with permission.

81. Mark 14:55.

82. Matthew 26:28.

83. The apostle Paul makes similar points, for example about God's promises being fulfilled in Jesus and about the link between Jesus' sacrifice and the new covenant (2 Corinthians 1:20 and 1 Corinthians 11:23–26).

84. From Cruz, N. with Buckingham, J., *Run Baby Run*, Hodder and Stoughton.

85. See Acts 17:22–31, especially verses 23, 24, 27, 29, and 30. Also, there is good evidence to support the statement that all three words, *theos*, *elohim*, and *allah*, have important usages outside the Christian, Jewish, and Islamic religions with which they are primarily associated. In the case of *elohim*, *el* was the high god in the Canaanite pantheon, *elohim* being the plural. In the cases of *theos* and *allah*, there are examples of pagan usages that predate Christian and Islamic ones.

86. Differences include the Christian view that he dwells in relationship with his people. See also Chapter 3, "Beliefs".

87. Chapman, C., *Cross and Crescent: Responding to the Challenge of Islam*, Leicester, Inter-Varsity Press, 1999, p. 229.

88. As a general rule, it is wise when working in different cultural contexts to respect the opinions of local indigenous Christian leaders about this.

89. For the purposes of this chapter, baptism refers to believer's baptism by immersion in water.

90. Not just a symbol, but certainly a symbol.

91. See for example Matthew 8:18–22 and Luke 14:25–33.

92. See for example Acts 9:18; 10:48 and 19:5.

93. From a conversation with David Devenish.

94. Much literature relevant to this discussion has been recently published, including Parshall, P., *Muslim evangelism: Contemporary approaches to contextualisation*, Milton Keynes: Authentic, 2003, or "Appropriate approaches in Muslim contexts", chapter by John Travis in *Appropriate Christianity*, Kraft, C. (ed.), California: William Carey Library Books, 2005. For a critical view of insider movements see www.insidermovements.org.

95. The literal meaning of *halāl* is "that which is solved or loosed".

96. The Oxford English Dictionary defines "idol" as "an image or representation of a god used as an object of worship", with "idolatry" being "worship of idols" (www.askoxford.com, accessed 19 November 2009). Islam expressly forbids images or representations of God, so according to this the Muslim God is not an idol. However, the Bible sometimes employs the theme of idolatry to refer to anything that diverts one's attention from the one true God, whom the Bible explains as having revealed himself in Jesus Christ. So, in this biblical sense the terminology does apply.

97. Wright, C., *The Mission of God: Unlocking the Bible's Grand Narrative*, Nottingham:IVP, 2006, pp. 179–187.

98. See Romans 1:18–32, where "when speaking of idolatry objectively as a phenomenon, Paul pulls no punches" (*The Mission of God*, p. 179).

99. Demetrius says of Paul's teaching in Ephesus, "He says that man-made gods are no gods at all" (Acts 19:26). See also Acts 14:8–20 (Lystra) and Acts 17:16–34 (Athens). *The Mission of God*, pp. 180–2.

100. See Amos 1:1 – 2:3 and Jonah 1:2 and 3:8 (*The Mission of God*, p. 185). Wright also positions Romans 1:18–32 within this prophetic category (p. 186).

101. I am grateful to Phil Moore for alerting me to this point.

102. Thanks to Nicole Ashton for alerting me to this.

103.   Wright, C., *The Mission of God*, p. 187 (his italics).

104. *Hamza* is generally not considered a full letter of the Arabic alphabet. So if you are ever asked how many letters there are in the Arabic alphabet, say twenty-eight and a half.

105. Huart C., Arabic Literature, London, 1903, p. 56 (I am grateful to Professor Geert Jan Van Gelder for this reference); Wightwick and Gaafar, Mastering Arabic, p. 65.

106. Thanks to Daphne Clifton for telling me about the phrase "weasel words".

107. However, in many non-Western cultures, the status of particular careers reflects well on the family, and parents see no problem in guiding (sometimes also pressuring) their children to follow such careers, for reasons of family honour. Witness the relatively high proportion of Indian doctors, lawyers, and accountants in the UK.

108. To find out more about the heritage, see Berkey, J. P., *Popular Preaching and Religious Authority in the Medieval Islamic Near East*, Seattle: University of Washington Press, 2001, pp. 36–52.

109. Lowry, E. L., *The Homiletical Plot: the Sermon as Narrative Art Form*, Westminster: John Knox Press, 2001.

110. See "Other resources" in Appendix 2.

Index